STEVEN MANN

D0000763

InfoPath® with SharePoint® 2010

HOW-TO

SAMS 800 East 96th Street, Indianapolis, Indiana 46240 USA

InfoPath with SharePoint 2010 How-To

ISBN-10: 0-672-33342-2

ISBN-13: 978-0-672-33342-2

Library of Congress Cataloging-in-Publication Data

Mann, Steve, 1950-

  InfoPath with SharePoint 2010 how-to / Steven Mann.

    p. cm.

  ISBN 978-0-672-33342-2

  1. Microsoft InfoPath. 2. Microsoft SharePoint (Electronic resource) 3. Business–Forms–Computer programs. I. Title.

  HF5371.M294 2011

  006.7'4–dc22

                                    2010041522

Fifth Printing: December 2013

Trademarks

Warning and Disclaimer

Bulk Sales

Pearson offers excellent discounts on this book when ordered in quantity for bulk purchases or special sales. For more information, please contact:

  U.S. Corporate and Government Sales
  1-800-382-3419
  corpsales@pearsontechgroup.com

For sales outside of the U.S., please contact:

International Sales
+1-317-581-3793
international@pearsontechgroup.com

Editor–in-Chief
Karen Gettman

Executive Editor
Neil Rowe

Acquisitions Editor
Brook Farling

Development Editor
Mark Renfrow

Managing Editor
Sandra Schroeder

Project Editor
Seth Kerney

Copy Editor
Keith Cline

Indexer
Cheryl Lenser

Proofreader
Apostrophe Editing Services

Technical Editor
Jason Barron

Team Coordinator
Cindy Teeters

Book Designer
Gary Adair

Page Layout
Bronkella Publishing

Contents at a Glance

Table of Contents

About the Author

Steve Mann was born and raised in Philadelphia, Pennsylvania, where he still resides. He is a principal architect for RDA Corporation and has more than 16 years of professional experience.

For the past seven years, he has primarily focused on collaboration and business intelligence solutions using Microsoft technologies. Steve managed the internal BI Practice Group at RDA for several years and is still an active participant. He is also heavily involved within RDA's Collaboration/Search Practice Group.

Steve enjoys vacationing with his family along the East Coast and usually visits three or four places each year, including locations such as Orlando, Florida; Williamsburg, Virginia; Ocean City, Maryland; Sea Isle City, New Jersey; and New York City.

Dedication

To my parents who always believed in me and have always been there for me.

To my wife, Pauline, who stood by me while I worked on this book.

To my wonderful children, Brittany, Emily, and Matthew, for understanding that Dad needed to work on his book.

Acknowledgments

Special thanks to Richard Phillips, one of my previous customers, who challenged me on InfoPath solutions within a SharePoint environment. Many ideas came from my experiences building solutions for Rich. Also, thanks to Gerald Crockenberg, Cindy Mocharnuk, and Kristin Kaempf, who assisted in the track-changes ideas and implementation; this is an awesome solution.

Thanks to RDA Corporation for supporting me on this book and assisting in its promotion.

Thanks to Sams Publishing and Brook Farling for making this book a reality and for giving me the opportunity to share my ideas and solutions.

Tell Us What You Think!

As the reader of this book, you are our most important critic and commentator. We value your opinion and want to know what we're doing right, what we could do better, what areas you'd like to see us publish in, and any other words of wisdom you're willing to pass our way.

I welcome your comments. You can email or write me directly to let me know what you did or didn't like about this book—and what we can do to make our books stronger.

Please note that I cannot help you with technical problems related to the topic of this book, and that due to the high volume of mail I receive, I might not reply to every message.

When you write, please be sure to include this book's title and author and your name and phone or fax number. I will carefully review your comments and share them with the author and editors who worked on the book.

Email: feedback@samspublishing.com

Mail: Neil Rowe
           Executive Editor
           Sams Publishing
           201 West 103rd Street
           Indianapolis, IN 46290 US

Introduction

Overview of This Book

With the latest release of Microsoft SharePoint Server 2010, the entire Office platform has become even more integrated than before. This does not leave out Microsoft InfoPath Designer 2010. There is a closer bond between SharePoint and InfoPath with the 2010 release.

This book is designed to cover all the aspects within InfoPath and SharePoint 2010 that relate to creating and developing business solutions. It is geared toward both technical and semitechnical professionals and does not require a degree in computer programming.

The scenario-based presentation of the material provides not only a great tutorial but also an in-depth reference for accomplishing integral InfoPath tasks within the SharePoint platform.

How to Benefit from This Book

We designed this book to be easy to read from cover to cover. The goal is to gain a full understanding of InfoPath with SharePoint 2010. The overall content can be considered a tutorial but can also serve as good reference material. Some material is an overview of functionality or features, but most of the content is hands-on or provides a hands-on view.

Keeping both beginners and experts in mind, this book provides both breadth and depth to the usage of InfoPath and can show you how to leverage it to create business solutions. We designed the content of this book so that it would appeal to a wide audience at various technical levels:

- ► Business analysts
- ► Information workers
- ► IT professionals
- ► IT developers
- ► Collaboration managers
- ► Content managers

You can access the code samples used in this book by registering on the book's website at **informit.com/register**. Go to this URL, sign in, and enter the ISBN to register (free site registration required). After you register, look on your Account page, under Registered Products, for a link to Access Bonus Content.

How to Continue Expanding Your Knowledge

We hope that this book provides foundational knowledge about InfoPath solutions with SharePoint 2010 and that you find everything you need here. However, business requirements and changing needs usually require custom solutions that cannot all be possibly documented in one location.

Therefore, the following resources are great ways to stay current and find additional answers if necessary:

- ▶ **Microsoft InfoPath Team Blog:** http://blogs.msdn.com/infopath/
- ▶ **Microsoft Office Developer Center:** http://msdn.microsoft.com/en-us/office/default.aspx
- ▶ **RDA Collaboration/Search Blog:** http://rdacollab.blogspot.com/
- ▶ **Author's Blog:** http://stevethemanmann.com/

CHAPTER 1

Usage of InfoPath Designer 2010

InfoPath is used to generate data entry forms for both the acquisition of information as well as storage of that information. With the 2010 release, InfoPath can now be used as an alternate way to present SharePoint 2010 content within the web browser, thus enhancing the overall user experience. Using forms with workflows can help manage and enforce business processes throughout an organization.

As always, you may easily create a form that can be rendered within SharePoint to handle the data entry of various business processes, such as a request for information, a suggestion box, or even a survey or review. The form may be submitted and saved within a form library. Workflows may act upon the saved form and perform various actions and approval processes (using information from the underlying libraries and lists).

SharePoint lists have various views for entering, editing, and viewing information within those lists. Previously, these were all system-based pages for forms. In the 2010 platform, these list forms can be modified or generated using InfoPath.

InfoPath can also access data from various data sources, including SharePoint itself. This provides great extensibility and consistency in providing data entry forms to the business. (For example, why repeat the same business data all over the place when you can get it from a central line-of-business system or SharePoint?)

Why Use an InfoPath Form?

An InfoPath form is a structured document that allows all users to enter different information the same way. The data entered into the form may be accessed and acted upon easily. This allows for the automation of business processes using the SharePoint Server environment.

Imagine using a Word document to handle requests. You would need a manual process of someone reading the document and then entering in the information into SharePoint or another system. Although this could be automated using a custom Office solution, using InfoPath 2010 eliminates this need.

> **NOTE**   For the technical folks, InfoPath 2010 is a fancy XML viewer. The resultant file from InfoPath is essentially a specialized XML document containing fields (metadata/schema) and values for those fields (data).

What Does InfoPath Do for My Lists?

The main storage within SharePoint is done through lists. Whether it be a document library, announcements, project status, or so on, they are all types of lists.

SharePoint enables users to interact with lists for entering items, viewing items, or modifying items. This is all done through the web browser based on the structure of the list.

In SharePoint 2010, the interface for interacting with these lists is done through forms. Therefore, you may use InfoPath 2010 to customize these forms and enhance the user experience.

In addition, you may modify the actual page used to render the form and use the InfoPath web part to further customize the overall presentation of that list.

Why Use InfoPath Forms in Workflows?

Because each form submitted may contain different selections or entered fields, a workflow can look at the InfoPath form entries and perform actions based on those entries.

It is easier to have a submitted form living in a form library and having a workflow process around that form than to submit emails with attachments and updates and-files get lost and nobody really knows where the latest version is located. InfoPath forms provide a centralized location for the information being acted upon.

How Does InfoPath Integrate with My Data?

InfoPath has the capability to receive and submit data to a variety of data sources. Therefore, you can capitalize on business functions that already exist (such as web services) to display data and to interface with custom-built databases or applications.

For standard business processes, creating a full-fledged web application for small transactions can be costly in resources and time. InfoPath 2010 combined with SharePoint 2010 makes it easier to create form-based interfaces that handle business data without full-time developers overengineering yet another web application that needs to be maintained and managed by the IT department (see Chapter 9, "Using Data in SharePoint Forms").

InfoPath Versus Web Controls and Web Parts

If you are a pro at ASP.Net and C#, you could easily generate web parts or web controls for SharePoint to create user inputs and display data from databases. With InfoPath, both developers and information workers can generate forms and data interfaces without writing code.

You may still actually use code to further enhance an InfoPath form, but that is not required to take advantage of most of the great features in InfoPath 2010.

What Is the InfoPath Web Part?

Microsoft Office SharePoint Server (MOSS) 2007 actually has a system-based InfoPath web part that it used to render forms within the browser. However, because it is system-based, it is hidden behind the scenes and therefore isn't available for general public consumption. SharePoint 2010 provides a user-based InfoPath web part that is available and ready to use. The web part enables the rendering of InfoPath forms within your SharePoint (see Chapter 10, "InfoPath Form Web Part").

Are There Any New Controls in InfoPath 2010?

Several new controls are available in InfoPath 2010. The picture button allows you to create button controls that are represented by a picture. Previously, there was no way to add a picture to your button or make a picture clickable.

The hyperlink control allows users to add a listing of hyperlinks to the form, and because most everything in SharePoint is a URL, this eliminates the need for attachments.

The people/group picker is now a real control within InfoPath, whereas previously you needed to find the Contact Selector ActiveX control within your local machine.

The date and time picker adds the time component to the date picker control to allow specific time entries. Previously, only the date picker was available, with no time element.

There is also now an external item picker that enables you to connect to external content types within SharePoint via the Business Connectivity Services.

In addition to the new controls, several preexisting controls are now available for browser-enabled forms, including the multiple-selection list box, the choice group and section, lists (bulleted, numbered, and plain), and the combo box control. Chapter 3, "SharePoint Form Controls," discusses the controls that are available for SharePoint forms.

Does InfoPath 2010 Make Anything Easier?

With the evolution of a software product, it is obvious that functionality and processes become easier and easier. The two most noticeable improvements from an ease-of-use standpoint are the quick-publish and quick-rules functionality.

Once a form is published, the publish configuration settings are stored such that any updates can be republished with a click of a button. Previously, each time you needed to publish a form, you were forced to step through the same wizard screens again and again when nothing actually needed to be changed.

The quick-rules functionality now brings menu-driven rules creation to InfoPath, enabling you to quickly create common rules specific to the selected controls. In addition, the new rules management pane allows you to copy and paste rules from one control to another, which makes the overall rule-creation experience easier and better than in InfoPath 2007.

Getting Started

To get started using InfoPath 2010, you need Microsoft Office Professional Plus 2010. Installing Microsoft Office Professional Plus 2010 allows you to choose InfoPath as one of the applications that gets installed. Once installed, your Windows Programs menu will include two links under the Microsoft Office folder: Microsoft InfoPath Designer 2010 and Microsoft InfoPath Filler 2010.

This book covers the use of Microsoft InfoPath Designer 2010 as that instance of InfoPath 2010 is the one which you use to design and create form templates. The Microsoft InfoPath Filler 2010 instance is the local instance of InfoPath which can be used to fill out forms that are not rendered through SharePoint (or a web browser).

For most, installing InfoPath 2010 locally on your computer will provide you the necessary means of accomplishing the tasks covered in these chapters. However, when developing code-behind that references the SharePoint assemblies, InfoPath 2010 must be installed in a SharePoint environment such as a virtual machine. The only solution in this book which that would be required is the Track Changes solution outlined in Chapter 18.

CHAPTER 2

Creating a SharePoint Form with InfoPath Designer

This chapter shows you how to generate an InfoPath form for use in SharePoint. The following chapters expand on the functionality and options available.

The first step to create SharePoint forms is to open InfoPath Designer. From there, you have a number of options. When designing a new form, you have the following template options:

▶ **SharePoint List:** Use this template to generate an interface for interacting with a SharePoint list. The generated form can create the actual list in SharePoint.

▶ **SharePoint Form Library:** Use this template to generate a form library that stores instances of your form from user input. The content type of this form library is your form template.

▶ **E-mail:** Use this template to generate a form that can be used within emails.

▶ **Blank Form:** This is the base web browser form template used to generate SharePoint forms from scratch.

▶ **Blank Form (InfoPath Filler):** This base client form template is used to generate forms that require users to have InfoPath installed locally on their computers. The forms created using this template are not rendered in a web browser.

▶ **Database:** Use this template to quickly create a form based on a database table from Access or SQL Server.

▶ **Web Service:** Use this template to generate a form that queries a web service for information.

▶ **XML or Schema:** This template is used to easily replicate the data structure of an XML file or schema (XSD).

▶ **Data Connection File:** Use this template to quickly generate a form that uses a data connection file stored in SharePoint.

▶ **Convert Existing Form:** The name is confusing, because you would think this is used to convert an existing InfoPath form, but this template actually uses converters to import Microsoft Word or Microsoft Excel documents and convert them into InfoPath forms.

▶ **Document Information Panel:** InfoPath now makes it easier to customize input into Office documents based on SharePoint columns. Use this template to generate the data entry portion of a Microsoft Office document that is stored within a SharePoint library and contains additional fields for user entry.

▶ **Blank 2007 Form:** Use this form to create a web-based InfoPath 2007 form.

▶ **Blank 2007 Form (InfoPath Filler):** Use this form to create a client-based InfoPath 2007 form. Users need InfoPath 2007 installed locally on their computers.

NOTE   Throughout this book, the terms InfoPath form and SharePoint form may be used interchangeably. A SharePoint form is essentially a web-enabled InfoPath form with the intention to be able to use the form in SharePoint.

Design a SharePoint Form Using the Blank Form Template

Scenario/Problem: You want to create a new form for user input to be used in SharePoint.

Solution: When you open InfoPath Designer 2010, you are automatically taken to the File, New page, as shown in Figure 2.1. Either double-click Blank Form or select the Blank Form button, and click the Design Form button to create a new blank form.

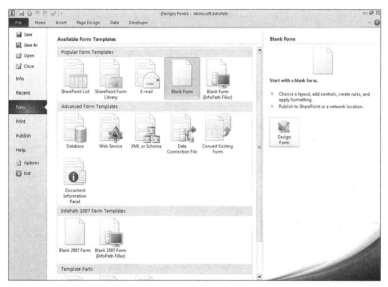

FIGURE 2.1
The New page provides templates for designing new forms.

To design a simple form, follow these steps:

1. Click the Click to Add Title text that appears and enter a title for the form.

2. Click in the bottom section of the form where it states Add Tables.

3. Click the Insert ribbon bar menu and select the Two-Column 4 table in the Tables section. This is a layout table that assists in aligning the labels and controls on your form.

4. Click the File menu and select Save.

5. Enter a name for the form file and click OK. This will save a local copy of the form.

We now have a base form to which we can start adding controls, as shown in Figure 2.2.

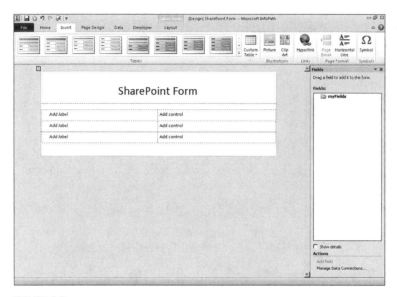

FIGURE 2.2
Entering a title and adding a layout table to a form produces a base form.

Add Controls

Scenario/Problem: You need to add controls to a form for user entry.

Solution: Use the Controls section from the Home top ribbon bar.

To add controls to your form, follow these steps:

1. Click the first Add Control cell in the layout table of the form.

2. From the Home ribbon bar, locate the Controls section, as shown in Figure 2.3, and click Text Box.

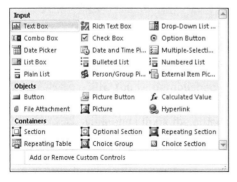

FIGURE 2.3
The Controls section displays the available controls that you can insert onto your form.

3. Click the Add label in the cell to the left of the text box and enter a label for this entry. This is tell the user what information to enter into the text box.

4. Repeat these steps for the remaining rows in the layout table. Your form should look similar to Figure 2.4

5. Click Save from the File menu to save your changes locally.

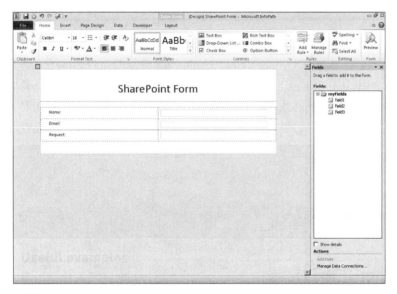

FIGURE 2.4
Adding labels and controls to the form provides the basis for user data entry.

Preview Your Form

Scenario/Problem: You need to see how your form works before you publish it to SharePoint.

Solution: With your form open and saved, there are three ways to preview the contents:

▶ Press the F5 key.

▶ Click the Magnifying Glass icon at the top of the InfoPath Designer application.

▶ Click the Preview Form button on the Home ribbon bar.

Your form will render in the InfoPath Filler version of the application, and you can view how it works there, as shown in Figure 2.5.

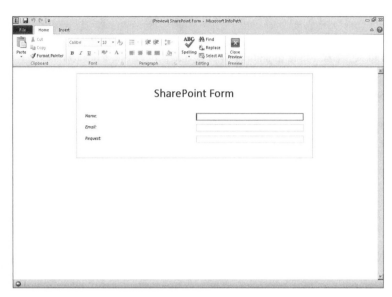

FIGURE 2.5
Previewing your form shows you how the user will experience it.

Name Your Data Fields

Scenario/Problem: You want to give your fields meaningful names. By default, when adding controls to your form, InfoPath names the fields that will store the data generically (that is, Field1, Field2, and so on).

Solution: Change the name of the each field by either right-clicking each control or right-clicking the fields in the Fields pane and selecting Properties. Enter a new name for the field name. Figure 2.6 provides an example.

To be consistent, naming conventions should be established. Developers may use camel case (for example, lastName, firstName), whereas business analysts might use Pascal case (for example, LastName, FirstName). There is no wrong answer as long as everyone follows the same standards.

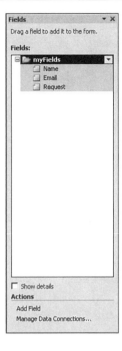

FIGURE 2.6
Naming your fields appropriately makes them easier to identify and manage.

Add Submit Options

Scenario/Problem: You need to enable users to submit the form after they fill it out.

Solution: From the File menu, select Info. On the Info page, click the Submit Form button.

Several options appear (as shown in Figure 2.7):

- ▶ To Email: Submitting this form will send the contents in an email to a specified address.

- ▶ To SharePoint Library: Submitting this form will send the contents as a saved instance of the form in a SharePoint form library.

- ▶ To Web Service: Submitting this form will send the form as XML to a web service.

- ▶ To SharePoint Server Connection: Submitting this form will use a specified data connection stored in SharePoint to submit the data.

- ▶ Submit Options: If you are familiar with InfoPath 2007 or just want to take control of the submit options, use this item menu to just get down to business.

FIGURE 2.7
Submit options determine where and how a completed form will be submitted.

For this scenario, let's just select To SharePoint Library. The Data Connection Wizard appears. For the form to be submitted to that form library, you need to have a data connection to the SharePoint library in the form.

You must specify a form library in SharePoint to submit the form; therefore, you might

TIP need to go to your SharePoint site and create a new form library first. Enter the location of the form library in the Document Library text entry. (Create a form

library named SharePoint Form for this example.)

You can create the form library right from InfoPath, as explained in a later section.

Now that some of the grunt work has been done, we come to the most important part of the submission to a document library: the filename. If you notice, by default, the filename is Form. That's great. If you leave it like that, only one person can submit the form, it will be called Form.xsn in the form library, and no one ever can submit the form again. Let's go home!

You need to specify something dynamic or unique about the form instance the user is submitting. This can be tricky. You must define a formula to implement this correctly, and although we haven't stepped through formulas yet, we are forced to do at least one here.

The main ingredients for specifying the filename correctly deal with either entries in the form or entries in the form combined with a system function such as the date.

For this example, we will use the name the user entered in the form along with a date function. To do so, follow these steps:

1. Click the Function button to the right of the File Name text box. The Insert Formula dialog appears.

2. Click the Insert Function button and select the concat function. Click OK. The function inserts three spots for you to modify.

3. Double-click the first entry and select the Name field from the field dialog that appears and click OK.

4. Only select the next entry (don't double-click) and replace it with " - ", including the quotes.

5. Select the last entry and click the Insert Function button. Select Today from the Date category.

6. Click OK.

7. Remove the Double-Click to Insert Field text if it still appears. Click OK. Your formula should now look similar to Figure 2.8.

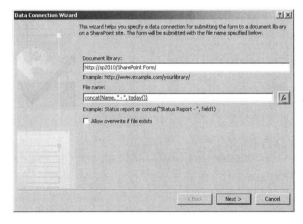

FIGURE 2.8
Using a formula for the file-name ensures that each instance is saved to a unique file.

8. Click Next. If you are prompted for credentials, enter them accordingly.

9. Click Finish to save the connection in the form.

TIP If you use the now date function, the time component will be used in the file-name, and even if you select to overwrite existing files, the filename will never be the same. Avoid this, if possible, because every update will generate a new file.

Publish Your Form

Scenario/Problem: You need to publish your form to SharePoint so that users can actually use it.

Solution: From the File menu, select Info. On the Info page, click Quick Publish.

Because we have gone through the submit options, InfoPath knows that the user will be submitting the form to a specific form library. Therefore, the submit location becomes the default publishing location; usually they are the same. Using the Quick Publish button, as shown in Figure 2.9, saves several steps (but we will still investigate manual publishing later). Note that the Quick Publish may not be available until a complete Publish has been performed once.

FIGURE 2.9

You can publish your form in one easy step by clicking the Quick Publish button.

Use Your Form in SharePoint

Scenario/Problem: You need to test your published form in SharePoint.

Solution: Navigate to the form library you created in SharePoint, and click the Add Document link.

Your form should render in the browser, as shown in Figure 2.10. Enter some values in the text boxes and click the Submit button. An instance of the form is saved to your form library, as shown in Figure 2.11. Notice the filename is using the formula we entered in our submit options.

NOTE   Using certain site templates, such as the Blank template, may not have Enterprise features enabled. You need to make sure Enterprise features are enabled to publish the form as a browser-enabled form.

NOTE   The Save and Save As buttons are shown here and will allow the user to save the form using a filename. This circumvents the configured Submit button. Chapter 8, "Submitting and Publishing in SharePoint," discusses how to change the buttons that appear.

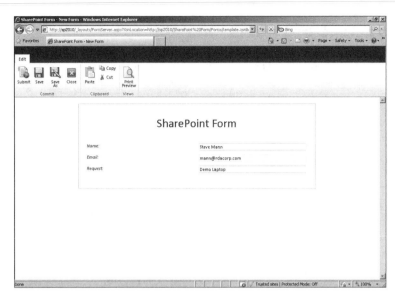

FIGURE 2.10
Clicking the Add document link opens a new instance of your form within the browser.

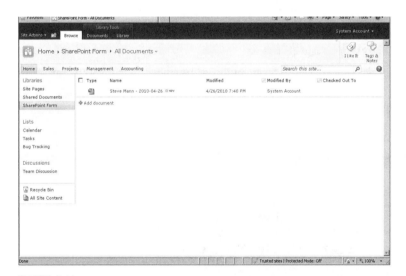

FIGURE 2.11
Submitting the form saves an instance of the form within the form library.

Create a Form Library from InfoPath

Scenario/Problem: You need to create a form library to publish and submit the form.

Solution: From the File menu, select Publish. On the Publish page, click SharePoint Server (Publish Form to a SharePoint Library).

In the previous section, you created the form library manually. By doing so, you understood where the InfoPath form was going to be published and submitted. When starting from scratch with the Blank Form template, you can use the Publish Form to a SharePoint Library option to create the form library and publish the form, but you also need to enter submit options after the form has been published. Therefore, you need to publish again after you have entered the submit options. It becomes a chicken-or-the-egg scenario.

Nonetheless, if you create a form using the Blank Form template, you may create the form library to house it using the Publish Form to a SharePoint Library option, as follows:

1. From the File menu, select Publish. On the Publish page, click SharePoint Server (Publish Form to a SharePoint Library). The Publishing Wizard appears.

2. Enter your main SharePoint URL or the full site address where you want the form library created and click Next.

3. Keep the defaults to create a form library and use the form in the web browser. Click Next.

4. Select the Create a New Form Library option, as shown in Figure 2.12, and click Next.

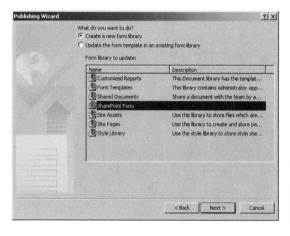

FIGURE 2.12

Selecting the Create a New Form Library option allows you to create the form library from InfoPath.

5. Enter the name of the new form library and a description on the next wizard dialog and click Next.

6. Click Next on the fields selection dialog.

7. Verify the information and click Publish.

Design a SharePoint Form Using the SharePoint Form Library Template

Scenario/Problem: You want to use the SharePoint Form Library Template to create a new form for user input in SharePoint.

Solution: From the File menu, select New. On the New page, click the SharePoint Form Library template button, and click the Design Form button.

The SharePoint Form Library template provides you with additional starting points, including two subheadings and tables, as shown in Figure 2.13.

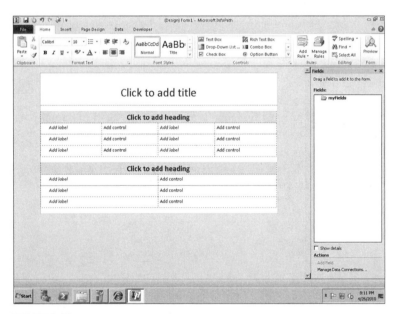

FIGURE 2.13
The SharePoint Form Library template provides more starting material for when you're designing a new form.

TIP The SharePoint Form Library template is a glorified version of the Blank Form template.

So, now you can use this template and apply the same techniques described earlier in this chapter to publish the form to SharePoint. You will still need to create a form library and configure the submit options.

CHAPTER 3

SharePoint Form Controls

Controls are items that you place on your forms to facilitate the data entry portion of the form. Some controls are what the user uses to enter the information (input controls), others are object controls such as a button, and yet other controls help contain others (container controls). All the controls available when generating a SharePoint form can be rendered within a web browser, but some controls can be used only within the filler forms. Because this book is for SharePoint 2010, we focus only on the controls that can be used within a web-based form.

The controls in InfoPath 2010 are categorized as follows:

▶ Input controls

▶ Object controls

▶ Container controls

This chapter briefly defines each of the controls in the preceding categories and describes various options that apply to each.

What Are Input Controls?

The input controls are used for data entry. They consist of a variety of types, including the following:

▶ **Text Box:** The most common control is a text box and allows the user to enter any alphanumeric characters. The data is stored as a string.

▶ **Rich Text Box:** An expansion of text box, this allows rich-text to be entered. Rich text may be formatted with fonts and colors. The data is stored as XHTML.

▶ **Drop-Down List:** The drop-down list control displays a listing of available items that the user may choose from. The underlying data has a display name and a value. The value is what is actually stored in the form. The data type can be any available data type but is usually a whole number (integer) that matches the identifier of the item that is selected.

▶ **Combo Box:** This control is a combination of a drop-down list control and a text box. It displays a list of available items, but it also allows the user to enter a new value that might not be in the list to choose from.

▶ **Check Box:** The check box stores a Boolean value that equates to whether the box is checked or cleared. The states can be True/False or 1/0 (or Blank for either state).

▶ **Option Button:** An option button is used in a set such that only one option may be selected within the set, with each having its own value. This is usually used when there are more than two options (otherwise a check box could be used) but not more than five or so (otherwise a drop-down list would be warranted).

▶ **Date Picker:** A date picker presents the user with a date entry mechanism along with a button to view a monthly calendar. The data may be configured to store a text value, date value, or date and time value.

▶ **Date and Time Picker:** Similar to the date picker, but this control comes with another text box for selecting the time portion of the date and time value.

▶ **Multiple-Selection List Box:** Presents a list of items to the user that are available for selection and provides a check box for each one, allowing more than one selection to be entered.

▶ **List Box:** Presents a list of items that the user may choose from. Similar to a drop-down, but the user sees a window of available items. If there are more items that fit within the control, scrollbars appear so that the user may scroll through the available options.

▶ **Bulleted List:** Allows a user to enter one or more items in a bulleted list format. The data may be stored using any data type, but the default is a string.

▶ **Numbered List:** Allows a user to enter one or more items in a numbered list format. The data may be stored using any data type, but the default is a string.

▶ **Plain List:** Similar to the bulleted or numbered list, but there are no bullets or numbers. The data may be stored using any data type, but the default is a string.

▶ **Person/Group Picker:** Allows for the selection of a specific user or group from SharePoint. The data stores a Person entry, but the main component is the account of the user (for example, domainusername).

▶ **External Item Picker:** Allows for the selection of data items from an external content type that has been configured in SharePoint using the Business Data Connectivity Services application.

What Are Object Controls?

The object controls allow for items to be placed on the form to assist in the use of the form. Here are the object controls available for a SharePoint form:

▶ **Button:** A normal Windows-type button used for some configured action such as submitting the form.

▶ **Picture Button:** A button that can present itself using a picture or icon. This may be used to enhance the aesthetics of the form and thus improve the user experience.

▶ **Calculated Value:** Presents a result from a formula on the form using functions and available form fields.

▶ **File Attachment:** Enables the user to attach an external file to the form.

▶ **Picture:** Allows users to add pictures to your form. The picture file is either embedded in the form or is accessed through a link.

▶ **Hyperlink:** Displays a hyperlink that will launch a new browser window when clicked. The user can modify the link on the form during data entry unless it is set to read-only.

What Are Container Controls?

The container controls allow for the grouping and management of other controls. The container controls available in a SharePoint form are explained here:

▶ **Section:** The main container control that can contain one or more input, object, or other container controls.

▶ **Optional Section:** This container does not display the controls within it unless the user is going to fill out the section (by clicking it).

▶ **Repeating Section:** Allows for multiple instances of the contained controls.

▶ **Repeating Table:** Allows for the data entry of multiple items that contain multiple columns.

▶ **Choice Group:** A control that contains choice sections.

▶ **Choice Sections:** These containers are used to optionally display sections (of controls) within a choice group.

Drag Controls on Your Form

Scenario/Problem: You cannot drag controls from the top ribbon bar onto your form.

Solution: Click the Controls Pane button on the Controls section of the Home ribbon bar to show the Controls task pane.

FIGURE 3.1

Clicking the Controls Pane button shows the Controls task pane.

Using the Controls task pane, you can drag controls onto your form instead of selecting and area and then clicking the control in the top ribbon bar.

FIGURE 3.2
An easier way to add controls to your form is to drag them from the Controls task pane.

Allow Users to Enter Text

Scenario/Problem: You need the user to enter text into a field on your form.

Solution: Drag a text box control onto your form.

The text box control allows the user to enter text (which is stored as a string) into a field.

Make a Text Box Read-Only

To make a text box read-only, follow these steps:

1. Right-click the text box control and select Text Box Properties to change the properties.
2. Click the Display tab, as shown in Figure 3.3.
3. Check the Read-Only check box.
4. Click OK.

Select this option if you want the text in the text box to be read-only. Use this only if you do not want the user to enter data into the field. In that case, the value of the text box should have a default value. This may be from a formula or from a data source field.

FIGURE 3.3
Checking the Read-Only check box locks your text box from data entry.

Make a Text Box Multiline

If you need to allow a user to enter multiple lines of text in a text box, the text box needs to be configured as a multiline text box.

To make a text box multiline, follow these steps:

1. Right-click the text box control and select Text Box properties to change the properties.

2. Click the Display tab.

3. Check the Multi-Line check box.

4. Click OK.

> **TIP** Once a text box is set to multiline, it is a good idea to expand the text box on the form so that users readily understand that multiple lines of text can or should be entered.

Allow Users to Select a Single Selection from a List of Items

> **Scenario/Problem:** You need the user to choose only one item from a list of defined values.

Solution: Drag a drop-down list box, list box, or combo box onto your form.

Any of the list box type controls allow you to display a set of values that the user may choose from. The controls in this section are considered single-select because they only allow one selected value.

The values may be entered manually, from another source in the form, or from a data source. We discuss hooking up controls to data in Chapter 9, "Using Data in SharePoint Forms," so for now let's enter values manually. To do this, follow these steps:

1. Drag a drop-down list box onto your form

2. Right-click the control and select Drop-Down List Box Properties. The Drop-Down List Box Properties dialog appears, as shown in Figure 3.4.

3. Click the Add button and enter a value and a display name in the Add Choice dialog, as shown in Figure 3.5.

FIGURE 3.4
From the Data tab on the Drop-Down List Box Properties dialog, you can populate your list with items.

NOTE   The example steps are for a drop-down list, but all list box type controls follow the same configuration.

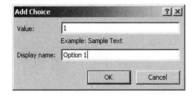

FIGURE 3.5
The Add Choice dialog allows you to add items to your list.

4. Repeat step 3 for additional items.

5. Click OK.

> **TIP** If there are many items to choose from, it is best to use the list box control and not a drop-down control.

Preview your form and you see that the drop-down list contains the items you entered, as shown in Figure 3.6.

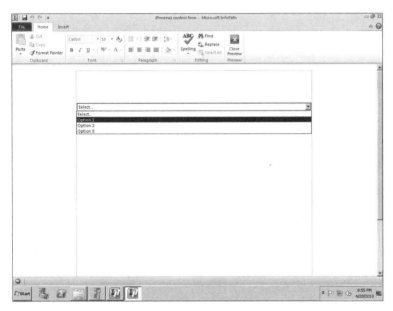

FIGURE 3.6
The drop-down list contains the items you configured it to contain.

> **TIP** If your value is not the same as the display name, you can test the value selected by dragging a text box onto the form and setting its default value to the field name of the drop-down list.

Allow Users to Select Multiple Items from a List of Items

> **Scenario/Problem:** You need the user to select from a list of defined values, and the user may choose multiple items.

Solution: Drag a multiple-selection list box onto your form.

The multiple-selection list box allows a user to select multiple items from the list of available items. The multiple-selection list box item display is configured the same as a single-selection list box control, but there are a few other options that are interesting.

By selecting the Allow Users to Enter Custom Values check box, as shown in Figure 3.7, you may allow users to enter their own values.

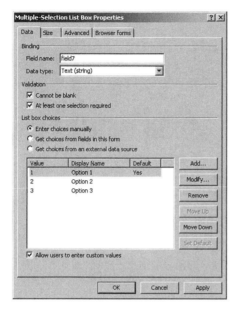

FIGURE 3.7

Check the Allow Users to Enter Custom Values check box if you want to allow users to type in a value to select.

To enforce that this field contains at least one value, check the At Least One Selection Is Required check box (also you may want to uncheck the default selection). When rendered, a red star will appear in the upper-right corner of the control area, as shown in Figure 3.8.

FIGURE 3.8

The red star in the list control indicates at least one selection is required.

This is different from most controls, where you would select only the Cannot Be Blank option, as explained in the "Make a Control/Field Required" section of this chapter.

The Cannot Be Blank option on the multiple-selection list box control is used to enforce that the custom value contains a value if selected, as shown in Figure 3.9.

TIP If you allow users to enter custom values, you should always select Cannot Be Blank regardless if at least one item needs to be selected. Otherwise, you might have a blank entry and not know whether the user forgot to, or just didn't want to, enter a value.

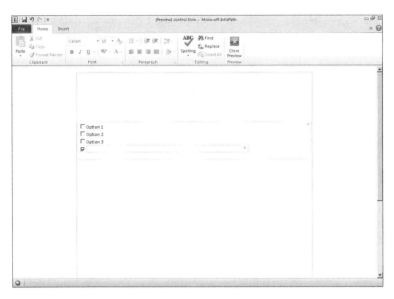

FIGURE 3.9
Selecting Cannot Be Blank forces the custom entry to have a value.

Allow Users to Select an Optional Single Choice

Scenario/Problem: You need the user to select an optional single choice.

Solution: Drag a check box control onto your form.

Use a check box when you have an optional value that the user can check off. The value is stored as a True/False (Boolean) data type.

TIP The field name that appears after placing a check box on your form is only a label and is not the configured field name. Just select the field name (for example, field2) and type the text the user should see.

To configure the check box properties, follow these steps:

1. Drag a check box control onto your form.

2. Right-click the control and select Check Box Properties. The Check Box Properties dialog appears, as shown in Figure 3.10.

3. Select the Checked option button if the check box should be checked by default.

4. Select the value when the check box is cleared.

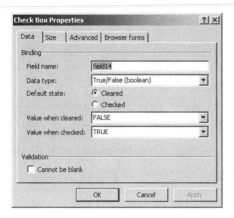

FIGURE 3.10
The check box properties allow you to config-ure the Boolean values.

5. Select the value when the check box is checked.

6. Click OK.

The values that you select may depend on how the consumer of the information will use those values or store them.

TIP Use reverse logic (for example, Checked=FALSE, Cleared=TRUE) if the consumer is asking the opposite question. For example, the check box might be to receive email notifications, whereas the list or destination value might be a flag to not send notifications.

Allow Users to Select from Various Options

Scenario/Problem: You need the user to select an optional single choice from multiple selections.

Solution: Drag an option button control onto your form and select the number of options.

When you select or drag an option button control onto your form, the Insert Option Buttons dialog appears, as shown in Figure 3.11

FIGURE 3.11
Entering the number of option buttons to insert places that many controls on your form.

Although this inserts multiple controls, they are all bound to the same field. The option that the user selects is the value that is entered in that field. The configuration for the option button is similar to the check box, but you need to configure each option button control.

To configure the option buttons, follow these steps:

1. Drag an Option Button your form.

2. Enter the number of option buttons. Click OK.

3. Right-click the first option button and select Option Button Properties. The Option Button Properties dialog appears, as shown in Figure 3.11.

FIGURE 3.12
From the Option Button Properties dialog, you can configure each option's values.

4. Enter the value for the first option button.

5. Check the This Button Is Selected by Default check box if you want this option button to be automatically selected.

6. Click OK.

7. Repeat steps 3-6 for the other option buttons.

> **TIP** Use option buttons when you have a static list of three to five items to choose from. Too many options would warrant a drop-down list. If you have only two options, consider whether you can use a check box.

Allow Users to Enter a Date/Time

> **Scenario/Problem:** You need the user to enter a date or date and time on your form.

Solution: Drag a date picker or date and time picker control onto your form.

The date picker and date and time picker present a text box with a calendar button for the user to select a date. The date and time picker displays an additional text box for the time component of the field.

The default data type for the date picker is date, but you may change this to date and time by configuring the properties and changing the data type, as shown in Figure 3.13.

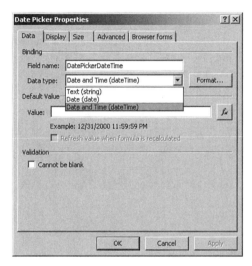

FIGURE 3.13
You can add the time element to the field by changing the data type of the date picker.

The date picker will still only show the date component to the user even if you change the data type, but the time component will be stored in the field. Figure 3.14 shows a form that demonstrates how each control is rendered and what value is stored.

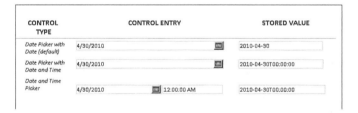

FIGURE 3.14
Using different date controls with different data types may or may not store the time value.

> **TIP** If the consumer of the form stores the date entry as a string, you should switch your date control's data type to Text to avoid any parsing conflicts.

Allow Users to Select a Person

Scenario/Problem: You need to allow the user to select a SharePoint user in your organization.

Solution: Drag a person/group picker control onto your form.

The person/group picker allows the user of the form to select a person who is a user within your SharePoint portal. The control presents a text box with an Address button and Check Names button for selection of users and confirmation of user entry, respectively.

This control has several configuration options. To configure the person/group picker control, follow these steps:

1. Right-click the person/group picker control on your form and select Person/ Group Picker Properties.

2. Open the SharePoint Server tab and enter the URL of your main SharePoint site, as shown in Figure 3.15.

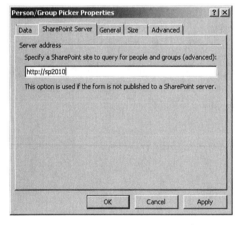

FIGURE 3.15
The SharePoint Server tab allows you enter the SharePoint site to select users.

3. Open the General tab. Here you have several options, as shown in Figure 3.16.

4. Select Allow Multiple Selections if the people/group picker should allow the user to select more than one person or group.

5. Select People and Groups if you want to allow the selection of both SharePoint users and SharePoint groups.

6. Select SharePoint Group and select a group from the drop-down to limit the SharePoint users (or groups) that are available to be selected.

7. Click OK.

FIGURE 3.16
The General tab determines which people can be selected and whether multiple selections are allowed.

Allow Users to Select from a SharePoint External Content Type

Scenario/Problem: You need to allow the user to select a value from a SharePoint external content type.

Solution: Drag an external item picker control onto your form.

The external item picker enables you to configure a connection to an external content type in SharePoint. The external content type is created and managed by the Business Data Connectivity services on your farm.

The external item picker requires many configuration steps, as discussed in Chapter 9.

Allow Users to Initiate an Action

Scenario/Problem: You need to allow the user to click an object to perform an action.

Solution: Drag a picture button or button object control on to your form.

The button object controls allow actions to occur when clicked by the user. The actions are configured using rules, which are discussed in Chapter 4, "SharePoint Form Rules."

TIP Use a picture button to enhance the aesthetics of your form.

You configure a picture button with an image. Alternatively, you may also configure a hover picture that displays when users hovers over the button with their mouse. To configure pictures for your image button, follow these steps:

1. Right-click the picture button control on your form and select Picture Button Properties. The Picture Button Properties dialog appears, as shown in Figure 3.17.

2. On the General tab in the Picture section, click the Browse button and select a picture file from your file system. Click Open.

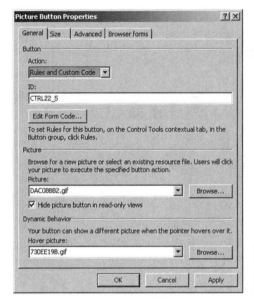

FIGURE 3.17
Configuring a picture button with a hover picture alerts the user that the image is clickable.

3. In the Dynamic Behavior section, click the Browse button and select a picture file from your file system that will be displayed when the user moves the mouse over the button. Click Open.

4. Click OK.

NOTE   Don't be alarmed by the name that is entered in the drop-down when you select an image file. InfoPath embeds the images into the form and designates a system name for them.

Show Optional Controls on Your Form

Scenario/Problem: You want to have optional controls display on the form but only if the user wants to enter the optional information.

Solution: Drag an optional section control container onto your form. Add the controls/fields that are associated with the optional section into the optional section control.

The optional section will, by default, show the controls it contains only if the user clicks the presented link, as shown in Figure 3.18.

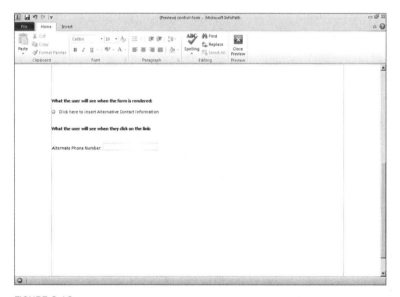

FIGURE 3.18
Clicking the Insert link displays the optional section to the user.

TIP To preserve screen real estate, use an optional section for items that won't be used often in the form.

Allow Users to Enter Multiple Instances of the Same Fields

Scenario/Problem: You want to enable users to enter multiple instances of information in a set of fields.

Solution: Drag either a repeating table or a repeating section control onto your form.

The repeating table presents fields in one or more columns and allows the user to insert multiple rows for data entry into the table, as shown in Figure 3.19.

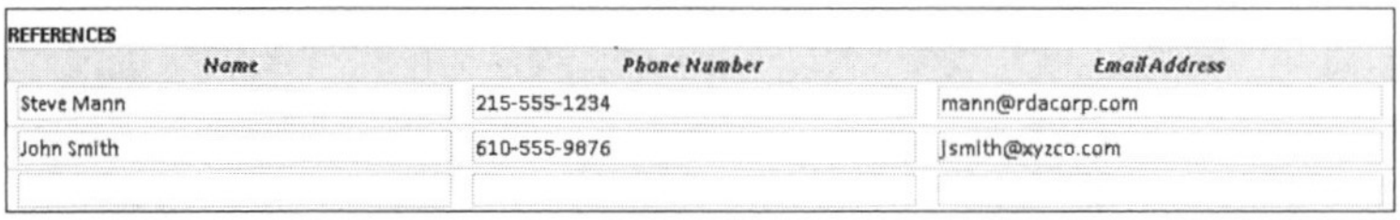

REFERENCES		
Name	*Phone Number*	*Email Address*
Steve Mann	215-555-1234	mann@rdacorp.com
John Smith	610-555-9876	Jsmith@xyzco.com

FIGURE 3.19
The repeating table allows the user to enter multiple rows of similar information.

The repeating section presents controls for user input and allows the user to add another instance of the section, as shown in Figure 3.20.

REFERENCES		
Name	*Phone Number*	*Email Address*
Steve Mann	215-555-1234	mann@rdacorp.com
John Smith	610-555-9876	Jsmith@xyzco.com

☑ Insert Item

REFERENCES

Name:	Steve Mann
Phone Number:	215-555-1234
Email Address:	mann@rdacorp.com

Name:	John Smith
Phone Number:	610-555-9876
Email Address:	Jsmith@xyzco.com

☑ Insert Item

FIGURE 3.20
The repeating section replicates the controls for the user to create a new entry.

Allow Users to Choose Which Set of Fields to Use

Scenario/Problem: You need the user to select which section of controls/fields to fill out.

Solution: Drag a choice group control onto your form, and enter controls into the choice sections.

Choice sections must be contained within a choice group. If you attempt to drag a choice section onto your form, it will appear inside a new choice group. When you place a choice group onto your form, two choice sections are automatically placed within the container, as shown in Figure 3.21.

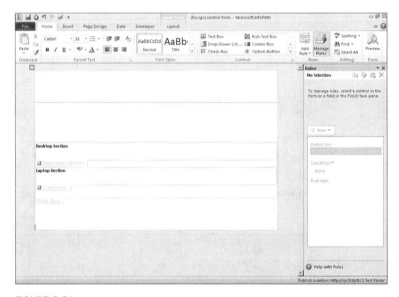

FIGURE 3.21
The choice group container allows multiple choice sections.

When the default section is rendered on the form, the user may remove or replace it with another, as shown in Figure 3.22.

TIP If the user selects the Remove menu option, the entire section is removed from the form. There is no way for the user to bring it back. Therefore, it is a good idea to disable the Remove menu option.

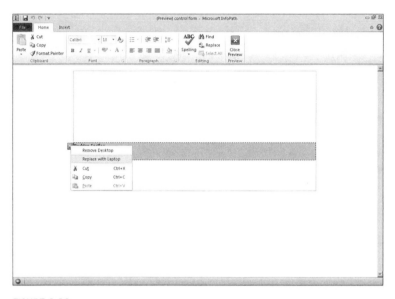

FIGURE 3.22
Using the section menu button, the user may replace the current section with another.

To modify the menu items that appear within the choice section, follow these steps:

1. Right-click the choice section and select Choice Section Properties. The Choice Section Properties dialog appears.

2. Click the Customize Commands button.

3. Select an action, and then modify the text in the Command name box, as shown in Figure 3.23. This is the text that appears in the section option menu.

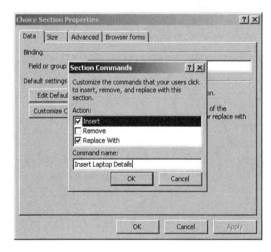

FIGURE 3.23
Customizing the commands determines what actions the user will see and how they will read.

4. Uncheck the Remove Action check box to disable the remove option. The Remove menu item will not appear when the user selects the option menu.

5. Click OK on the Section Commands dialog.

6. Click OK on the Choice Sections Properties dialog.

7. Repeat steps 1-6 for each additional choice section.

> **NOTE** The Insert command is not applicable to the Choice section as the user is selecting between one of the available choices and not actually inserting a new instance of the section.

Make a Control/Field Required

> **Scenario/Problem:** You need to make sure the user enters a value or makes a selection for a particular field.

Solution: Check the Cannot Be Blank check box within the properties of the control.

Within each control's properties, on the Data tab, there is a Validation section that contains a check box labeled Cannot Be Blank. Checking this checkbox will enforce the need for a selection or entry by the user. The form will not be allowed to be submitted until an entry is made.

CHAPTER 4

SharePoint Form Rules

This chapter explains how to create rules and discusses various scenarios where rules apply. Using rules in your SharePoint form helps bring your form to life and provides a more interactive experience with the user.

Rules are ways you can add intelligence to your form without actually coding. Rules use conditions to determine when they should function. The functioning of a rule is called an action.

You may use rules to hide controls, sections, and so on based on certain conditions. You can also use rules for custom validation. Adding actions to buttons involves rules, as well. Without rules, you would need to be a .NET developer to handle even the simplest logic.

Hide or Show Controls Based on a Selected Option

Scenario/Problem: You need to hide or display controls based on a user selection.

Solution: Group the controls within a section and add a formatting rule to the section.

This will probably be one of the first things you need to do on your form that requires a rule. It works similarly to an optional section, but you control when the section appears based on a user selection. Formatting rules not only apply to font styles but also have the option to hide a control or disable a control.

For this scenario, we will use a check box and a section of controls, as shown in Figure 4.1. When the check box is checked, we want show the controls; otherwise, they should be hidden.

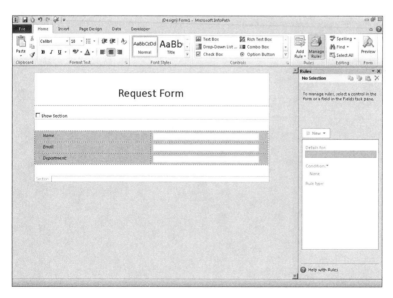

FIGURE 4.1
Adding controls within a section assists in changing the visibility.

Because we will be hiding or showing the section, we need to add the rule to the section. Here are the steps:

1. Select the section of controls you want to hide and show.

2. Click Manage Rules on the Home tab of the ribbon bar. The Rules pane appears, as shown in Figure 4.2.

FIGURE 4.2

The Rules pane allows you to manage the rules for the selected control.

3. Click the New button and select Formatting from the drop-down list.

4. Replace Rule 1 as the name with Hide.

5. Under the Condition section, click the None link. The Condition dialog appears, as shown in Figure 4.3.

FIGURE 4.3

Adding conditions builds the logic for your rule.

6. In the first drop-down, select Select a Field or Group. The Select a Field or Group

> **TIP** Click the Add button to string together multiple conditions together using AND or OR logic. You cannot use parentheses, so it is better to use all ANDs or all ORs. You are allowed up to five condition entries.

7. dialog appears, as shown in Figure 4.4.

FIGURE 4.4

The Select a Field or Group dialog allows you to make selections outside of the section control.

8. Select the field that will control the visibility of the section. In this example, the check box is bound to the showSection field. Click OK.

9. In the third drop-down box of the Condition dialog, select FALSE. Your condition dialog should now look like Figure 4.5. Click OK.

FIGURE 4.5

When the check box is not checked (FALSE) the condition will be met.

> **TIP** To determine which conditions to enter, think about the action that will be taken and when you want that to occur. In this case, when the check box is not checked, we want to hide the control. Because the formatting option is to Hide the Control (not Show the Control), think about when you want the section hidden.

10. Finally, back in the Rules pane, click the Hide This Control check box. Your rule should now appear as in Figure 4.6.

Preview your form to test out the rule. The section should not appear at first. When you click the check box, the rule should kick in and a Controls section should appear.

> **TIP** Use the same logic to hide or show sections using other types of controls, such as an option button or drop-down list.

FIGURE 4.6
The configured rule details appear in the Rules pane.

Format an Entry Based on a Condition

Scenario/Problem: You want to change the font style of an entry based on that entered value.

Solution: Add a formatting rule to the control that is configured to change the font properties.

A classic example that fits in this scenario is changing a negative number to a red color. Therefore let's use a text box that is used to enter numbers, as shown in Figure 4.7. The field is configured to display in Decimal format, and by clicking the Format button, you can change the display format to Currency.

To configure the formatting rule for the Amount field, follow these steps:

1. Select the Amount text box and click Manage Rules on the ribbon bar(from the Home tab). The Rules pane appears. (If the Rules pane is already shown then clicking Manage Rules again will close it).

2. Click New in the Rules pane and select Formatting.

3. Click the None link in the Condition section. The Condition dialog appears.

4. In the Condition dialog, select Is Less Than in the second drop-down.

FIGURE 4.7
Configuring a text box as decimal allows for currency entry and display.

5. In the third drop-down, select Type a Number, and then enter 0 into the text box that appears over the drop-down, as shown in Figure 4.8. Click OK.

FIGURE 4.8
Selecting Type a Number allows you to enter a value into the third option

6. Back in the Rules pane, select the font color in the Formatting section, as shown in Figure 4.9. For this example, we will change the font color to red.

7. Save and preview your form. An example preview is shown in Figure 4.10.

FIGURE 4.9
In the Formatting section, you can specify which font styles will be applied.

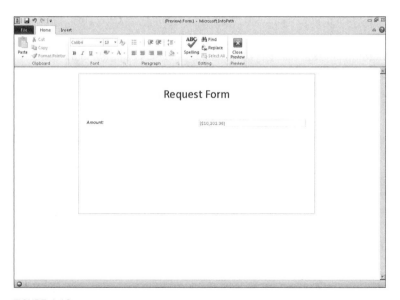

FIGURE 4.10
Entering a negative value turns the font color to red.

Implement a Validation Rule

Scenario/Problem: You need to validate the entered value of a field.

Solution: Add a validation rule to the control/field

Let's build upon the previous scenario. The form is a request form, so the amount has to be more than zero (although showing a red negative number did look nice). You will need to add a validation rule to the Amount field.

> **TIP** Validation rules prevent your form from being submitted with wrong values.

To make sure the value is greater than zero, follow these steps:

1. Select the Amount text box and click Manage Rules on the ribbon bar(from the Home tab). The Rules pane appears.

2. Click New in the Rules pane and select Validation.

3. Enter a new name for the rule.

4. Click the None link in the Condition section. The Condition dialog appears.

5. In the Condition dialog, select Is Less Than or Equal To in the second drop-down.

6. In the third drop-down, select Type a Number, and then enter 0 into the text box that appears over the drop-down. Click OK.

7. Enter a screen tip, such as Must be greater than zero. Your rule configuration should look similar to Figure 4.11.

> **TIP** The conditions for validation rules should be the ones that make the entry invalid. Reverse logic thinking applies here. In our example, we wanted values greater than zero, so we added a validation rule for values that were less than or equal to zero.

8. Save and preview your form. An example preview is shown in Figure 4.12.

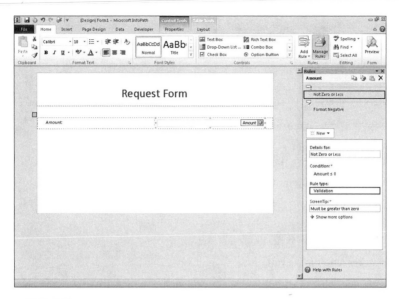

FIGURE 4.11
Validation rules are applied based on the condition.

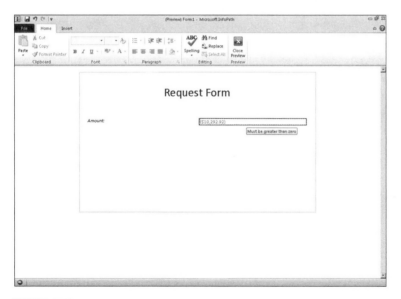

FIGURE 4.12
Entering a value less than or equal to zero produces a validation error.

Add an Action Rule to a Button

Scenario/Problem: You need to perform an action when the user clicks a button.

Solution: Add an action rule to the button.

An action rule, as its name implies, performs an action. While this scenario uses a button control, action rules may be applied to other types of controls as well.

To add an action rule to a button, follow these steps:

1. Select the button on your form and click Manage Rules on the ribbon bar. The Rules pane appears.

2. Click New in the Rules pane and select Action.

3. Enter a new name for the rule.

4. Click Add and select an action to take, as shown in Figure 4.13.

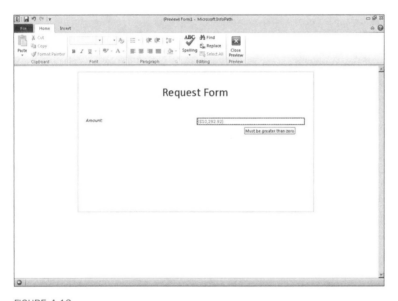

FIGURE 4.13
Selecting the action will determine what the button performs.

5. A Rule Details dialog will appear. The dialog options depend on which action is selected. An example Rules Detail dialog is shown in Figure 4.14. Configure the action and click OK.

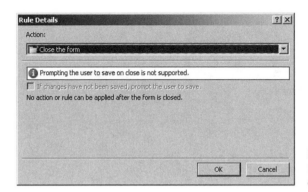

FIGURE 4.14
Use the Rules Detail dialog to
configure the action.

TIP There is no need to configure a condition on a button, because the rule is fired when clicked. If you need a condition, think about moving that rule to the control or field that is involved.

Use Rules for Form Submission

Scenario/Problem: You want to perform actions during the submission of your form

Solution: Configure submit options to use rules and then configure form submit rules.

The form submit rules allow you to enter one or more rules (or actions) to handle the submission of your form instead of just letting the form get submitted using the Submit connection.

Before you use the rules, you first need to configure the submit options in the form as follows:

1. On the Data ribbon bar, click Submit Options. The Submit Options dialog appears.

2. In the Submit Options dialog, select the Perform Custom Actions Using Rules option, as shown in Figure 4.15. (Make sure the Allow users to submit this form checkbox is selected).

3. For this example, click the Advanced button and change the After Submit to Leave the Form Open, as shown in Figure 4.16.

4. Click OK.

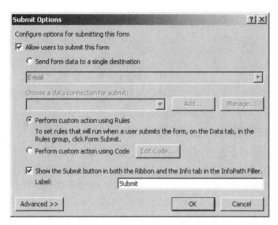

FIGURE 4.15
Submit options allow you to configure the submission of the form.

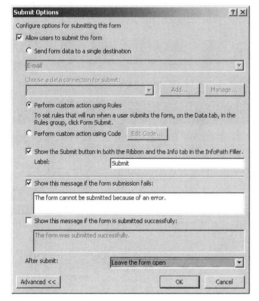

FIGURE 4.16
The After Submit option determines
what happens after submission.

That takes care of the submit options, but now you need to configure the form submit
rule. For this example, you will need to create a new view (see Chapter 6, "SharePoint
Form Page Design and Views") named Close View, which should contain a message
and a button that closes the form. (Sneak a peek at Figure 4.21 to get an idea about
this.)

To enter the submit rule, follow these steps:

1. On the Data ribbon bar, click Form Submit in the Rules section. The Rules pane
   appears.

2. Click New and select Action.

3. Enter Submit Form as the name of the rule.

4. Click Add and select Submit Data. The Rule Details dialog appears, as shown in Figure 4.17.

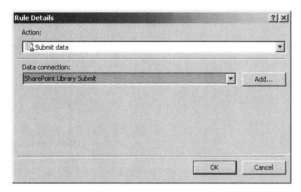

FIGURE 4.17
Configuring the connection determines where it will be submitted.

5. Select the data connection to submit the form. (If you don't have a data connection configured, see Chapter 2, "Creating a SharePoint Form with InfoPath Designer," for an example.) Click OK.

NOTE The Form Submit button on the Data tab in the ribbon will be disabled if the Submit Options are not set to Perform custom action using Rules.

6. Click Add again to add another action. Select Switch Views. In the Rules Details dialog, change the view to Close View, as shown in Figure 4.19. Click OK.

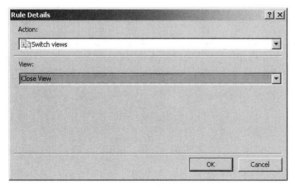

FIGURE 4.19
Selecting a view determines which one will be displayed.

7. Save and publish your form to SharePoint. Once your form is published to SharePoint, you may create a new instance and test the rules. Submitting the form will save a copy and display the close view, as shown in Figure 4.21.

FIGURE 4.21
Submitting the form saves an instance in the library and changes the view.

Use Rules for Form Loading

Scenario/Problem: You want to perform initial action

Solution: Configure form load rules.

ns when the form is rendered

The form load rules are executed when the form is loaded. If you need to set initial values or perform other actions before the user enters data into your form, this is where those actions are configured.

To add rules for form loading, follow these steps:

1. On the Data ribbon bar, click Form Load in the Rules section. The Rules pane appears.

2. In the Rules pane, click New and select Action.

3. Enter a name for your rule.

4. Select the action you want to perform. The Rule Details dialog appears.

5. Configure the rule details and click OK.

6. Add a new rule or additional actions as needed.

Validate Data Entry Using Patterns

Scenario/Problem: You need to ensure that the entered value of a field (such as an email address or phone number) is properly formatted.

Solution: Use the pattern-matching condition in your rule.

There are built-in patterns that you can use to validate data entry on your form. Two of the most common ones, email and URL, are available in the Add Rules shortcut menu items when a control is selected.

When selecting a condition from the Add Rules menu, you must choose an action or formatting rule to create, as shown in Figure 4.24. The pattern-matching rule is created with two conditions, as shown in Figure 4.25.

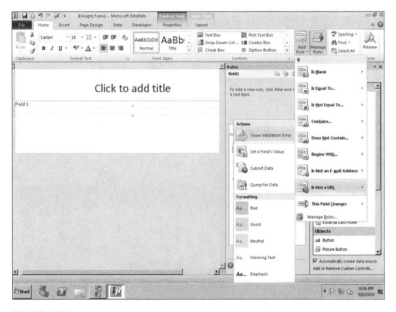

FIGURE 4.24
Selecting the action or formatting from the side menu creates the rule.

Click one of the conditions to see how they are configured. The Condition dialog shows both conditions for the rule.

TIP Whereas the Add Rules button allows you to quickly generate common rules, creating rules from scratch helps you understand what you are creating; use the Add Rules button to generate examples to learn from.

FIGURE 4.25

Creating a rule from the Add Rules menu autopopulates the conditions and screen tip.

Select the third drop-down (which currently shows URL) and select the Select a Pattern option. Bingo! The Data Entry Pattern dialog appears, as shown in Figure 4.26. It's almost like finding a hidden treasure.

FIGURE 4.26

Configure the Data Entry Patterns dialog to define valid entries.

As you can see, there are six prebuilt patterns and an option to create a custom one. Use the Insert Special Character drop-down to assist in generating a custom pattern.

For example, if you want to make sure a dollar amount is between $0.00 and $9.99 and is entered with the dollar sign, you can create the pattern $d.dd, as shown in Figure 4.27.

FIGURE 4.27

The Example line in the dialog helps you preview the pattern.

CHAPTER 5

SharePoint Form Functions

This chapter explores the various functions that are available within InfoPath. Functions enable you to manipulate, construct, or obtain data within your form. Functions can be used throughout InfoPath in the following areas:

- Default values for fields/controls

- Calculated value control

- Naming the form instance on submission

- Rules

Use the SharePoint URL Functions

Scenario/Problem: You need to obtain the SharePoint URLs where the form is published.

Solution: Use the built-in URL functions.

The URL functions provide you with absolute SharePoint URLs for the following locations:

- List URL: The SharePoint list URL where the form is published

- Server Root URL: The root SharePoint server URL

- Site Collection URL: The SharePoint site collection path where the form is published

- Site URL: The SharePoint site path where the form is published

The respective functions are shown in Figure 5.1.

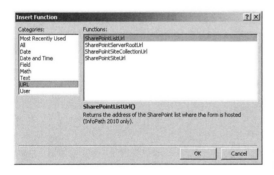

FIGURE 5.1
Selecting URL displays the available SharePoint URL functions.

To demonstrate the differences in the functions and paths, an example form was published to a form library, in a team site, located in a site collection within the /sites/ managed path of the root server site collection. To make this easier, the form library exists at http://sp2010/sites/SiteCollection/TeamSite and is named Form Library (for originality of course).

When using the SharePoint URL functions on a form at the location described, you should see the following values:

- ▶ List URL: http://sp2010/sites/SiteCollection/TeamSite/Form Library/

- ▶ Server Root URL: http://sp2010/

- ▶ Site Collection URL: http://sp2010/sites/SiteCollection/

- ▶ Site URL: http://sp2010/sites/SiteCollection/TeamSite/

Let's look at that example form in SharePoint (see Figure 5.2).

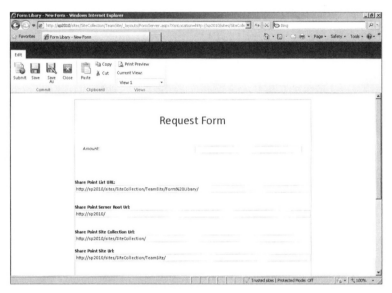

FIGURE 5.2
Using the SharePoint URL functions helps gain key path information.

> **TIP** SharePoint URL functions come in handy when using workflows or other areas where you need to link to locations in your SharePoint portal.

Calculate a Future Date

> **Scenario/Problem:** You need to automatically create a future date (such as a due date) that is x days from today (or other date).

Solution: Use the addDays() with the today() function or a form date field.

Date functions are common in business application forms, especially those involved in workflows. To calculate a date in advance, use the addDays function, which takes a date as the first parameter and a number of days as the second parameter.

So if you needed to figure out 30 days from today, you would use addDays(today(), 30), as shown in Figure 5.3.

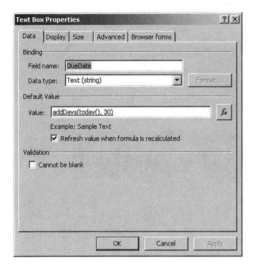

FIGURE 5.3
Adding days to today produces the future date which is x days from now.

If you have another date field on your form (in a date picker for example), you can easily use that as your reference date rather than today() by inserting that field into the addDays() function. An example is shown in Figure 5.4.

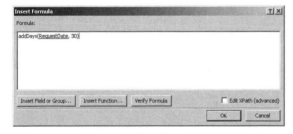

FIGURE 5.4
Using a field value in the addDays() function produces a future date based on another user entry.

Get the Current SharePoint User

Scenario/Problem: You need to know which SharePoint user is using the form.

Solution: Use the userName() function.

The username() function returns the account name of the current SharePoint user. A great example where this can be used is within a people/group picker control. The people/group picker control produces a repeating Person group that contains fields related to the user account. You want to locate the AccountID field, as shown in Figure 5.5.

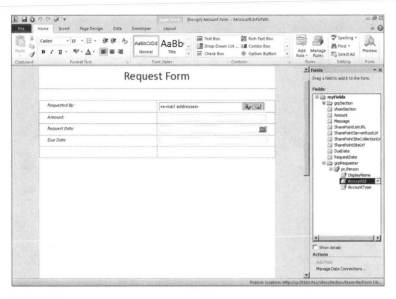

FIGURE 5.5
Using the people/group picker produces a special repeating group of fields.

Set the default value of the AccountID field to `username()`, as shown in Figure 5.6.

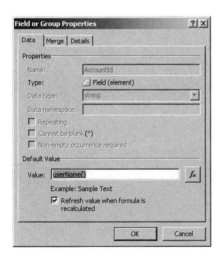

FIGURE 5.6
Using the userName() will default the entry to the user filling out the form.

When the form is rendered, the people/group picker will display the current username in the text box, as shown in Figure 5.7.

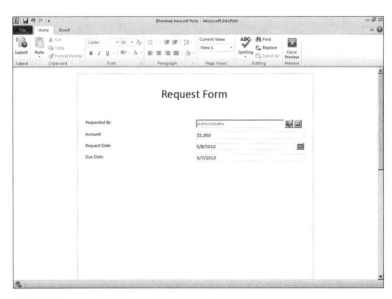

FIGURE 5.7
The result of the userName() function is presented in the people/group picker.

Notice the name is in red. The account is not validated. This can be easily corrected by using the userName() function again for the DisplayName field. You may also default the AccountType to the text value of User. Figure 5.8 shows the results of the doing so.

FIGURE 5.8
Defaulting both the DisplayName and AccountID to userName() allows the user account to be validated.

> **TIP** When a SharePoint group is selected in the people/group picker, the AccountType is set to SharePointGroup. When an AD group is selected, the AccountType is set to SecurityGroup. You may use this field to know what kind of account was entered.

Remove Leading and Trailing Spaces from a Field Value

> **Scenario/Problem:** You need to make sure there are no leading or trailing spaces in the field value.

Solution: Use the normalize-space() function with the field to normalize.

The normalize-space() function removes all spaces from the beginning and end of a field value that is used with the function. Insert the field you want to normalize in the function, as shown in Figure 5.9.

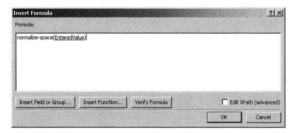

FIGURE 5.9

Entering a field in the normalize-space() function will remove spaces from that field value.

> **TIP** It is always good to normalize field values that come from data connections to ensure there are no extra spaces. Text box entries from the user are automatically normalized.

Remove All Spaces from an Entry

> **Scenario/Problem:** You need to use the entered value without spaces.

Solution: Use the translate() function to replace the spaces with an empty string ("").

The translate() function is a replace function that substitutes characters with replacement characters. However, by using an empty string, the translate() function removes the characters. Therefore, to remove all spaces from a value, use the translate() function to find all spaces and replace them with nothing, as shown in Figure 5.10.

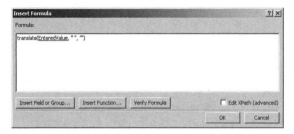

FIGURE 5.10
Replacing a character with an empty string removes the occurrence of that character.

Figure 5.11 shows a preview of the results.

Request Form

Requested By:	Administrator
Amount:	$0
Request Date:	5/8/2010
Due Date:	2010-06-07
Entered Value:	This is the entered value
No Spaces Value:	Thisistheenteredvalue

FIGURE 5.11
Using translate() to remove spaces sets the field to the entered text without the spaces.

Default a Blank Amount to Zero

Scenario/Problem: You need to ensure that at least a zero is entered into an Amount field and it is not left blank.

Solution: Use the nz() function.

The nz() function will default a field value to zero if it is left blank. This comes in handy when you need to calculate values or if a data connection can't accept a blank value. Simply use the nz() function and insert the field that contains the value, as shown in Figure 5.12.

Previewing the results is shown in Figure 5.13.

FIGURE 5.12
Using nz() ensures the value will
not be blank.

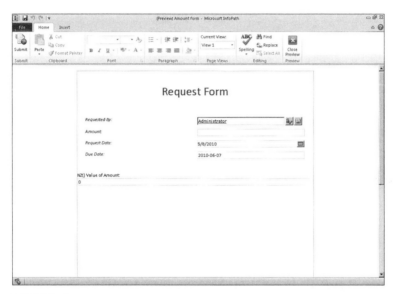

FIGURE 5.13
Leaving the Amount field blank makes the nz() function produce a zero.

TIP Use the nz() function on a field itself instead of enforcing a rule or validation
that cannot be blank. This will be one less error the user can make, assuming that
having a zero in the field is an acceptable value.

Calculate the Sum of All Items

Scenario/Problem: You need to calculate a total sum for multiple numeric
entries in your form.

Solution: Use the sum() function against the repeating group's Amount field.

The sum( ) function will total the values of entered within a group of fields. For this
example, we will use a repeating table that contains request items. Each request item
has an Item and ItemAmount field, as shown in Figure 5.14.

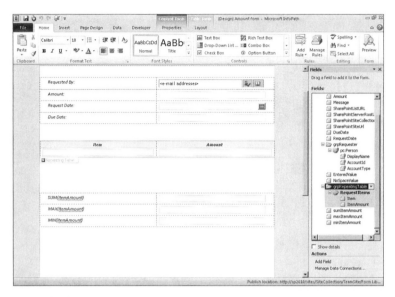

FIGURE 5.14
Creating a repeating group assists in performing math functions.

We will set another field on the form to use the sum() function against the ItemAmount, as shown in Figure 5.15.

Preview the form and enter values into the repeating table, as shown in Figure 5.16. The sum() function totals all amounts entered.

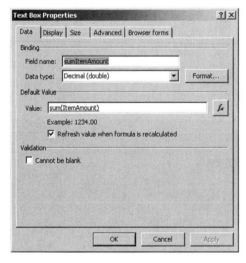

FIGURE 5.15
Using the sum() function against a repeating group's amount field will total all values entered for each item

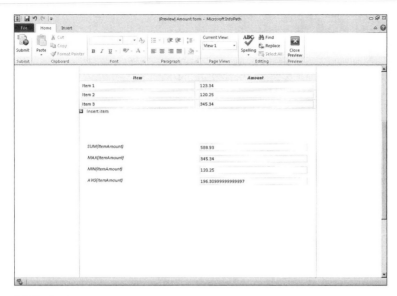

FIGURE 5.16
Entering items in the repeating table allows the sum() function to produce a running total

---

TIP You may use min(), max(), and avg() in the same way as sum(). The preview figure in this section shows examples of their outputs.

Determine a Count of the Items Entered

Scenario/Problem: You need to know how many items have been entered into a repeating group.

Solution: Use the sum() function against the repeating group's amount field.

The count() function will return the number of items entered within a repeating group. For this example, we will expand the example used in the previous section. For count() to work, it must be applied to the repeating group, as shown in Figure 5.17.

Placing a field on the form that contains this function will show the number of items entered, as shown in Figure 5.18.

NOTE The count() function will return how many items exist regardless if they contain values.

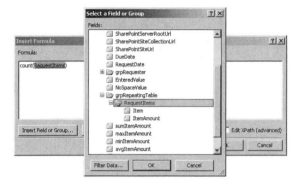

FIGURE 5.17

Inserting the repeating group field into the count() function produces the number of items in the group.

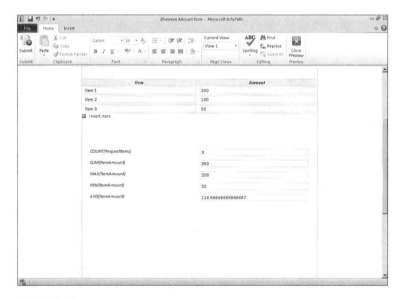

FIGURE 5.18

Entering new items into the repeating group increases the count.

Obtain a Portion of an Entered String

Scenario/Problem: You need to parse out or only grab a portion of an entered text value.

Solution: Use one of the substring() functions.

The substring() functions enable you to grab a portion of the string value that was entered. The functions available are as follows:

▶ Substring(text, start position, character count): The `substring()` function returns the string from the text field starting at the start position and ending based on the character count.

▶ Substring-After(text, find text): The `substring-after()` function returns the string in the text field after the specified characters.

▶ Substring-Before(text, find text): The `substring-before()` function returns the string in the text field before the specified characters.

You may also combine the `substring()` function with the `string-length()` function to determine how many characters to return as shown in Figure 5.19.

Previewing the results of the `substring()` functions are shown in Figure 5.20.

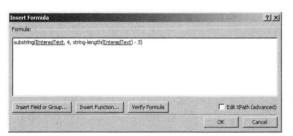

FIGURE 5.19
Using string-length() with substring() allows you to strip off a beginning number of characters.

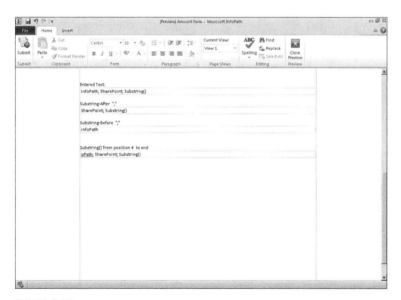

FIGURE 5.20
Using the substring() functions returns only portions of the entered value.

CHAPTER 6

SharePoint Form Page Design and Views

This chapter explores the various page design options available in InfoPath and how to create different views. Several examples and scenarios throughout this book use views to change the appearance of the form.

The page design of your form can be modified by using the Page Design and Layouts ribbon bars. The Page Design bar includes Views, Page Layout, Themes, and Header/Footer options. The Layout bar contains options for modifying tables within the form.

Change the Current View Name

Scenario/Problem: You want to change the current view name.

Solution: Click the Properties button within the Views section on the Page Design ribbon bar, as shown in Figure 6.1.

FIGURE 6.1
Clicking Properties allows you to modify the view settings.

Clicking Properties displays the View Properties dialog box shown in Figure 6.2. Enter a new name and click OK to change the name of the current view.

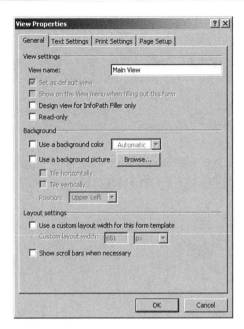

FIGURE 6.2

Entering a new name changes the current view's name.

Create a New View

Scenario/Problem: You need to present an alternative view of your form to the user.

Solution: Click New View within the Views section on the Page Design ribbon bar.

Clicking New View presents the Add View dialog, as shown in Figure 6.3. Enter a name and click OK to create the new view.

FIGURE 6.3

Entering a name and clicking OK creates a new view.

TIP   Create a new view to generate a print version of your form!

Change the Default View

Scenario/Problem: You want to switch the default view.

Solution: Select the view from the View drop-down, and click Properties within the Views section on the Page Design ribbon bar.

The default view is the view of the form that will display when the user opens a new or existing form. From the View Properties dialog, check the Set as Default View check box, as shown in Figure 6.4, to make the current view the default view.

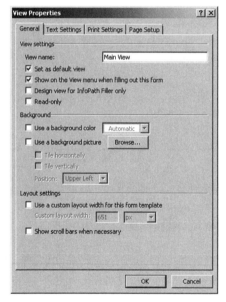

FIGURE 6.4
Checking the Set as Default View check box makes the current view the default view.

NOTE   If the view that you are editing is already the default view, the option to make it the default view will be disabled. Essentially, InfoPath won't let there be a state where no view is the default.

Make a View Read-Only

Scenario/Problem: You need to have a view in which users cannot make any changes.

Solution: From the View Properties dialog, click the Read-Only check box, as shown in Figure 6.5.

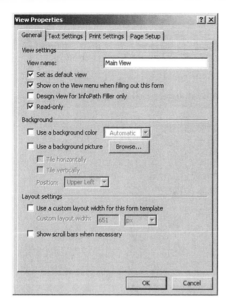

FIGURE 6.5
Checking the Read-Only check box locks the form and doesn't allow any edits to occur.

Prevent a User from Selecting a View

Scenario/Problem: You don't want a view to be available to the user.

Solution: From the View Properties dialog, unselect the Show on View Menu When Filling Out This Form option, as shown in Figure 6.6.

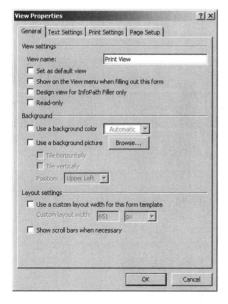

FIGURE 6.6
Unselecting the Show on View Menu When Filling Out This Form option makes the view unavailable for user selection.

In addition to this option, if you don't want the user to have the ability to select a view at all, follow these steps:

1. From the File menu, select Info, and then click the Form Options button.

2. On the Form Options dialog, under the Web Browser category, uncheck the Views option within the Show Commands section, as shown in Figure 6.7.

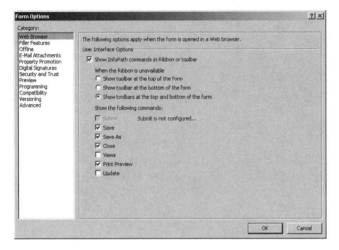

FIGURE 6.7
Unselecting the Views command option removes the ability for the user to change views of the form.

Use a View for Printing

Scenario/Problem: When printing your form, you always want a certain view to be used.

Solution: From the View Properties dialog, in the Print Settings tab, select your print view in the Designate Print View section, as shown in Figure 6.8.

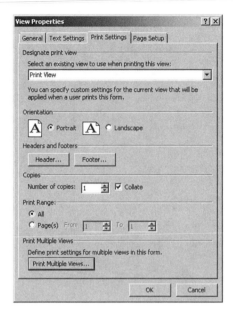

FIGURE 6.8
Designating a view for printing will insure that the print view is always used.

Use a Different Layout for Your Form

Scenario/Problem: You need to change the layout from the default layout when creating a new form.

Solution: Select a new layout from the Page Layout & Templates button on the Page Design ribbon bar.

Several layouts are available for your new form, as shown in Figure 6.9. The default for a blank form is Title Only.

TIP Because selecting a layout adds that selection to your form, you might find it easier to select everything and delete it before applying a new template.

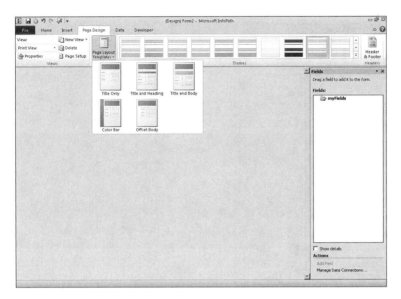

FIGURE 6.9
Selecting a page layout assists in the initial creation of your form.

Use a Theme for Your Form

Scenario/Problem: You want to choose a nice colorful theme for your form.

Solution: Select a new theme from the Themes section of the Page Design ribbon bar, as shown in Figure 6.10.

There are so many different themes to choose from. The most important aspect is the background color of the tables that contain your controls and labels. This is represented in the bottom half of the theme previews.

> **TIP** Being a SharePoint-related book, you would think that the SharePoint themes would be recommended. Although it is easy to just say that, it is a matter of personal preference and company policy. Use any theme that suits your needs and preference. Also note that using a custom table may not reflect a selected theme.

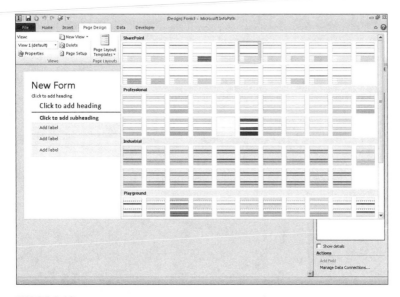

FIGURE 6.10
Selecting a theme determines what background colors are used within your tables and form.

Add Headers/Footers to Your Form

Scenario/Problem: You need to add headers or footers to your form when the form is printed.

Solution: Click the Header & Footer button on the Page Design ribbon bar.

The Header & Footer button is just a quick link to the View Properties, Print Settings tab. Click the Header or Footer button on the dialog to modify the header or footer of the printed form, as shown in Figure 6.11.

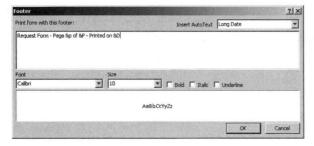

FIGURE 6.11
Adding text and auto text to your header or footer provides additional information when printing your form.

Insert a Table Layout into Your Form

Scenario/Problem: You need to insert a table into your form.

Solution: From the Insert ribbon bar, choose a table layout from the Tables section, as shown in Figure 6.12.

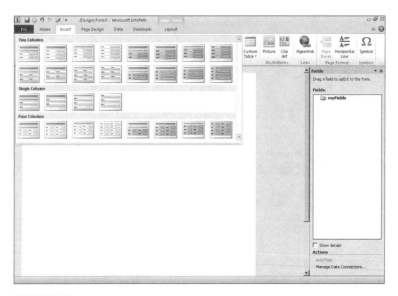

FIGURE 6.12
Selecting a table layout helps implement the structure of your form.

Modify a Table Layout in Your Form

Scenario/Problem: You need to make modifications to a table in your form.

Solution: Use the Layout ribbon bar.

The Layout ribbon bar contains a multitude of options for your form table, as shown in Figure 6.13.

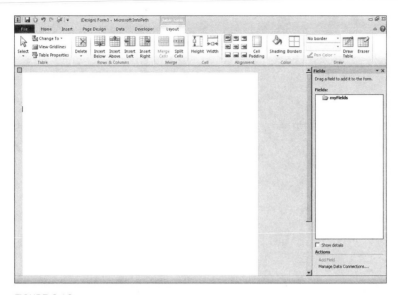

FIGURE 6.13
The Layout ribbon bar enables you to make various table modifications.

CHAPTER 7

SharePoint List Forms

This chapter explores how to use InfoPath with SharePoint 2010 to generate and customize lists within your sites. In the 2010 platform, the integration between InfoPath and SharePoint has been greatly improved. The scenarios here explain how to take advantage of this integration.

Use a Form to Create a SharePoint List

Scenario/Problem: You need to create a form to be used within a SharePoint list that doesn't exist yet.

Solution: Click File, New, and then select the SharePoint List form template, as shown in Figure 7.1. Click the Design Form button.

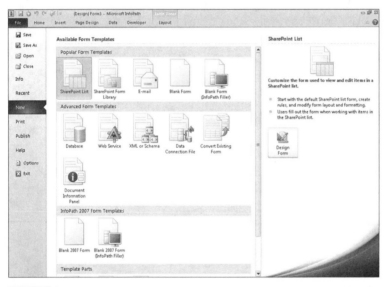

FIGURE 7.1
Using the SharePoint List form template allows you to create the SharePoint list using the form.

Instead of having to create a list in SharePoint and then customizing the form, you may actually design a form and have it create the SharePoint list directly through InfoPath Designer. This aids in streamlining both the list and form creation.

From the solution step, clicking the Design Form button initiates the Data Connection Wizard, as shown in Figure 7.2.

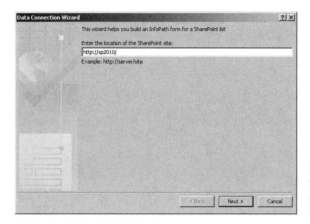

FIGURE 7.2
The Data Connection Wizard
assists in creating a form for a
SharePoint list.

To configure the data connection using the wizard, follow these steps:

1. Enter the URL of your SharePoint site where you want the list created. Click Next.

2. Enter the name of the list you want to create, as shown in Figure 7.3. Click Next.

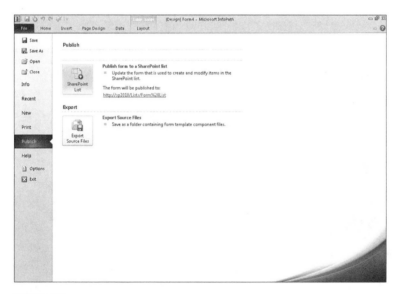

FIGURE 7.3
Entering a list name will create a new list using that name.

3. Optionally, check the Manage Multiple List Items check box to use the form to edit more than one list item, as shown in Figure 7.4. Click Finish.

The form is generated, and the list is created with the main system default fields. You can see the fields in the Fields pane, as shown in Figure 7.5.

> **TIP**   Click Show Advanced View at the bottom of the Insert a Field box to show the form fields as displayed in the figures.

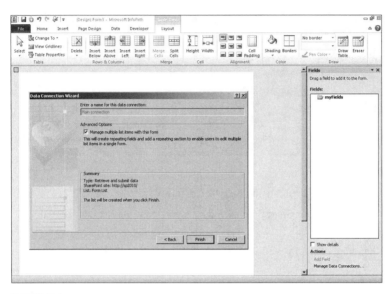

FIGURE 7.4
Selecting the Manage Multiple List Items option prepares the form to handle data from more than one list item.

FIGURE 7.5
Creating the new list for the form generates the system default fields.

You may add additional fields and controls to your form as needed for your list. The SharePoint list will be updated, and any new fields will be created upon publishing. An example is shown in Figure 7.6.

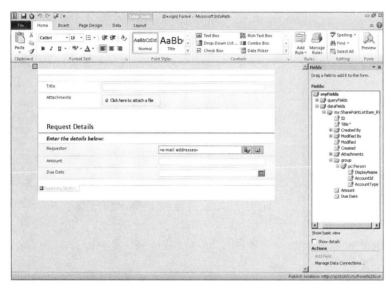

FIGURE 7.6
Adding new fields and controls updates the SharePoint list when publishing.

To add additional fields and controls to your form, follow these steps:

1. From the File, Publish page, click SharePoint List to publish the form to SharePoint, as shown in Figure 7.7.

2. Navigate to the list in SharePoint and click Add New Item to review your form changes, as shown in Figure 7.8.

TIP Use the link in the publish confirmation message to easily navigate to the SharePoint list.

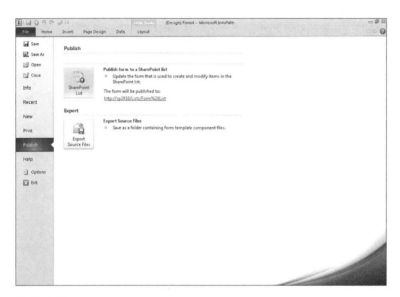

FIGURE 7.7
Publishing the form to the SharePoint list updates the list that was configured.

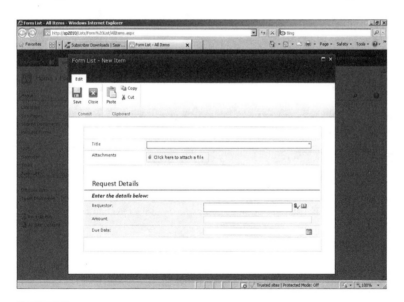

FIGURE 7.8
Adding a new item to the list uses your form to obtain the values of the list item.

Modify the Form of an Existing SharePoint List

Scenario/Problem: You need to change the form that is used within an existing SharePoint list.

Solution: There are two ways that this may be accomplished. The first is to edit the form from SharePoint, and the second is to open the form from InfoPath. You are still using InfoPath in both cases.

A great improvement in SharePoint 2010 is the ability to customize the form of a SharePoint list. The integration with InfoPath 2010 allows you to load the form for editing right from the SharePoint ribbon.

To edit the form from SharePoint, follow these steps:

1. Navigate to the list in which you want to edit the form.

2. On the List ribbon bar, click Customize Form, as shown in Figure 7.9.

3. Modify the form as desired and publish back to SharePoint.

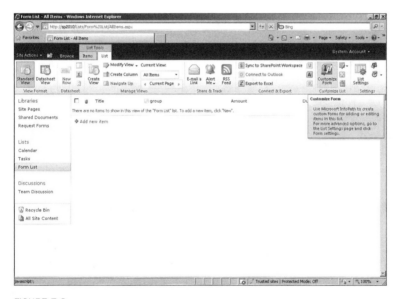

FIGURE 7.9
Using the List ribbon bar allows you to edit the form for the current list.

TIP An alternative method from SharePoint is to click the Form Settings from the List Settings administration page.

To edit the form from InfoPath, follow these steps:

1. From InfoPath Designer, click File, New.

2. On the New page, select SharePoint List and click the Design Form button.

3. Enter the SharePoint server URL on the Data Connection Wizard and click Next.

4. Select the Customize an Existing SharePoint List option and select the list you would like to modify, as shown in Figure 7.10. Click Next.

5. Click Finish. The current list form opens in the designer.

6. Modify the form as desired and publish back to SharePoint.

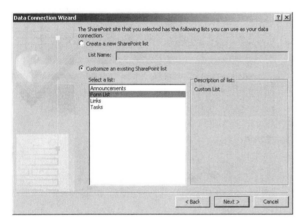

FIGURE 7.10
Selecting the list opens the current list form template for modification.

> **TIP** These steps are similar to creating a new list except this time you are choosing to modify an existing list.

Set Your List Form Template Back to the Default Form

> **Scenario/Problem:** Your modified form didn't turn out so well, and you want to go back to the default system form for that list.

Solution: Click Use the Default SharePoint Form option under Form Settings of the list.

Once you modify a list form, you do not need to live with it forever. Fortunately the system default form does not get overwritten or replaced. You have the ability to revert back to the default form for the list.

The steps to set your list back are as follows:

1. Navigate to the list in SharePoint.

2. On the List ribbon bar, click List Settings, as shown in Figure 7.11.

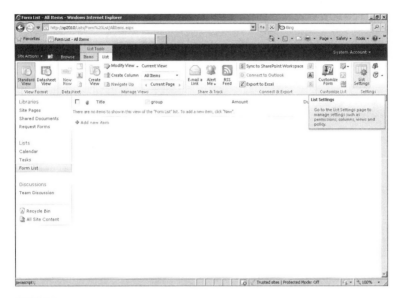

FIGURE 7.11
Clicking List Settings navigates to the List Settings page.

3. Click the Form Settings link at the bottom of the first column.

4. Select the Use the Default SharePoint Form option and optionally check the Delete the InfoPath Form from the Server to remove the form that you modified, as shown in Figure 7.12.

5. Click OK.

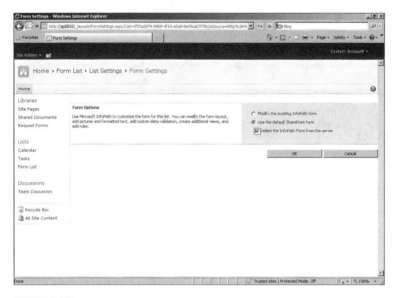

FIGURE 7.12

Clicking Use the Default SharePoint Form reverts the list form template back to the default form.

CHAPTER 8

Submitting and Publishing in SharePoint

IN THIS CHAPTER

- ▶ Enable Your Form for Submission
- ▶ Configure Email Submission
- ▶ Publish Your Form to Email
- ▶ Configure SharePoint Library Submission
- ▶ Publish Your Form to a SharePoint Library
- ▶ Use Multiple Forms in SharePoint Libraries
- ▶ Configure Web Service Submission
- ▶ Configure SharePoint Server Connection Submission
- ▶ Modify the Available Menu Buttons During Form Submission

This chapter covers the various submission and publishing capabilities when using InfoPath 2010 with SharePoint 2010. Although submitting and publishing are two different things, they are similar in that you are sending information to SharePoint in some way.

The submit options are used to configure how the user will submit the form when it is completed. The publishing options are how you deploy your form for general use. We discussed some of this in earlier scenarios, so let's cover all the options and steps here.

Enable Your Form for Submission

Scenario/Problem: You need to allow users to submit your form.

Solution: Click Submit Options and select the Allow Users to Submit This Form option.

The first step in configuring the submission of your form is to enable users to the submit form. To do this, follow these steps:

1. Select the Data ribbon bar and click the Submit Options button, as shown in Figure 8.1.

2. On the Submit Options dialog, check the Allow Users to Submit This Form option, as shown in Figure 8.2.

3. Configure the submission details accordingly (explained in this chapter).

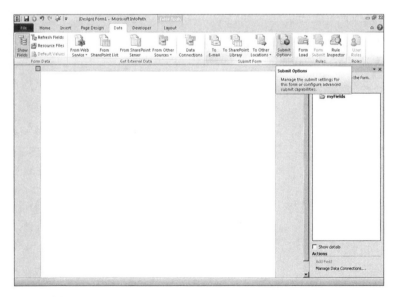

FIGURE 8.1
Clicking the Submit Options allows you to configure your form submission.

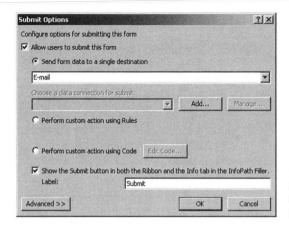

FIGURE 8.2
Selecting the Allow Users to Submit This Form option enables form submission.

Configure Email Submission

Scenario/Problem: You need your form to be submitted via email.

Solution: Click Submit Options and configure the email settings.

Continuing from the previous scenario, after you allow users to submit your form, the Send Form to a Single Destination option becomes enabled. The first option is Email, so you don't have to change anything in the drop-down. However, you must choose a data connection to use with the email submission. Chances are you don't have one yet, so let's create that now.

To configure the email connection, follow these steps:

TIP Quickly get to the email connection settings by clicking the To Email button on the ribbon bar instead of Submit Options.

1. Click the Add button on the Submit Options dialog. The Data Connection Wizard for the email connection appears, as shown in Figure 8.3.

2. Enter values for at least To and Subject. Click Next.

3. Choose Send Only the Active View of the Form and No Attachment, as shown in Figure 8.4. Click Next.

NOTE If you submit the form as an attachment, the actual .xsn file will be attached to the email. The person receiving the form must have InfoPath Filler 2010 on his computer to open the attached form.

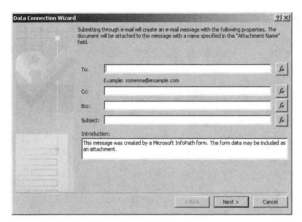

FIGURE 8.3
Filing in the fields defines the email properties.

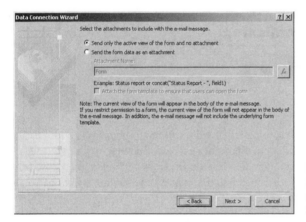

FIGURE 8.4
Sending only the active view doesn't require InfoPath Filler 2010.

4. Enter your desired data connection anem and click Finish on the summary screen, as shown in Figure 8.5.

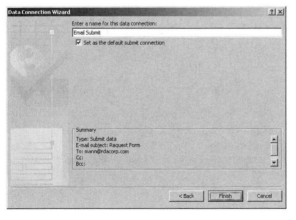

FIGURE 8.5
Clicking Finish creates your email submission data connection.

> **NOTE**   To submit using email from SharePoint, the outgoing email settings in SharePoint must be enabled and configured.

The email that is sent to the recipient has the form embedded, as shown in Figure 8.6.

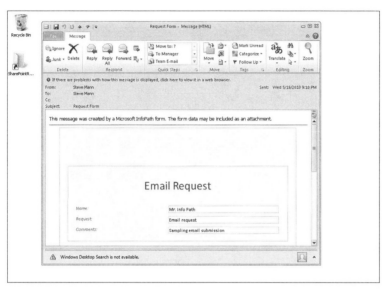

FIGURE 8.6
Submitting via email embeds the form contents into the email body.

Publish Your Form to Email

Scenario/Problem: You need your form to be filled out via email.

Solution: Publish your form to users via email using the Email publish option.

In the previous scenario, the form was submitted via email. The form appeared as read-only and wasn't filled out by the recipient. In this scenario, you want the users to fill out the form via email and submit from the email itself.

To accomplish this, simply follow these steps:

1. From File, Publish, click the Email button, as shown in Figure 8.7.

2. In the Publishing Wizard, enter a name for your form, as shown in Figure 8.8. Click Next.

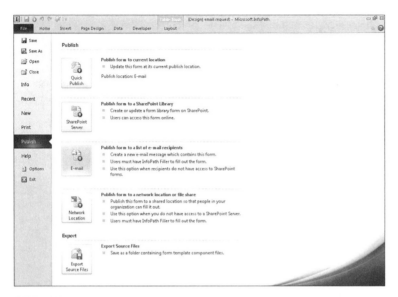

FIGURE 8.7
Clicking the Email button allows you to publish the form to email recipients.

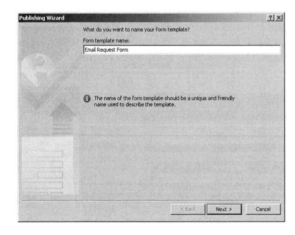

FIGURE 8.8
Entering a friendly template name helps identify the form being published.

TIP Publish your SharePoint forms (via email) to people that don't have access to your SharePoint site.

3. Click Next on the property promotion page.

4. Click Publish. The form publishes to Outlook, and a new email is presented with your form, as shown in Figure 8.9.

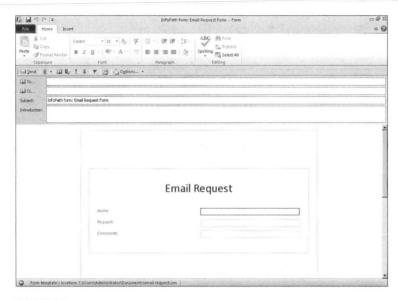

FIGURE 8.9
The publishing to email process produces the actual email to send to recipients.

5. Enter the email addresses of the people to send this form to and click Send (just like a regular email).

6. Your form email is sent to the users you specified. A user can fill out your form right within the email, as shown in Figure 8.10.

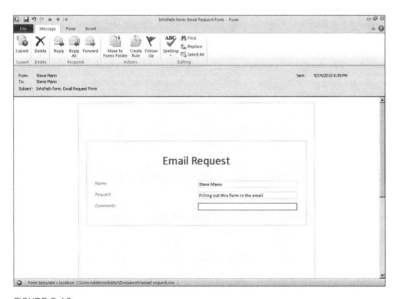

FIGURE 8.10
Publishing to email allows the users to fill out the form in the email itself.

Configure SharePoint Library Submission

Scenario/Problem: You need your form to be submitted and saved to a library on your SharePoint site.

Solution: Click Submit Options and configure the document library settings.

Continuing from the enable form submission scenario, after you allow users to submit your form, the Send Form to a Single Destination option becomes enabled. Change the setting to SharePoint Document Library, as shown in Figure 8.11.

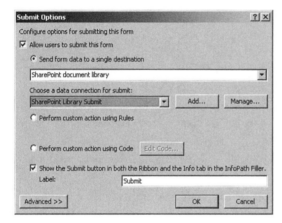

FIGURE 8.11
Selecting the SharePoint document library configures the form to submit to a SharePoint library.

Select a data connection that has been configured to a SharePoint library. If your form doesn't have one yet, you will need to configure a new SharePoint library connection.

TIP Quickly get to the SharePoint library connection settings by clicking on the To SharePoint Library button on the ribbon bar instead of Submit Options.

To configure the SharePoint library connection, follow these steps:

1. Click the Add button on the Submit Options dialog. The Data Connection Wizard for the SharePoint library appears, as shown in Figure 8.12.

2. Enter the document library URL and a dynamic form name. (See Chapter 2, "Creating a SharePoint Form with InfoPath Designer," for a discussion about creating the formula for the form name.) Click Next.

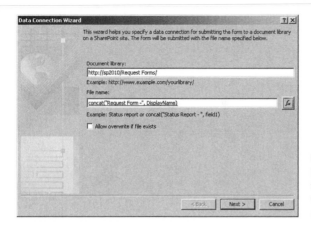

FIGURE 8.12
Entering the library URL and the form name tells InfoPath where to submit it and what to name the (form) instance.

3. Enter a name for the connection and Click Finish.

4. Back on the Submit Options dialog, make sure your new connection is selected and click OK.

Publish Your Form to a SharePoint Library

Scenario/Problem: You need your form to be filled out from a SharePoint library.

Solution: Publish your form to the SharePoint library.

In the previous scenario, you configured the submission of your form to a SharePoint library. Now you need to publish your form to SharePoint (typically to the same library).

To accomplish this, simply follow these steps:

1. From File, Publish, click the SharePoint Server button, as shown in Figure 8.13.

2. In the Publishing Wizard, enter the location of the SharePoint library, as shown in Figure 8.14. Click Next.

TIP The URL that you enter technically only needs to be the URL of the site that contains the form library where you want to publish your form.

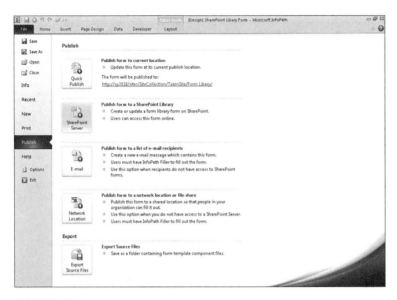

FIGURE 8.13
Clicking the SharePoint Server button allows you to publish the form to a SharePoint library.

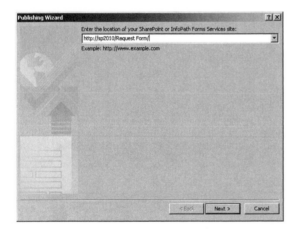

FIGURE 8.14
Entering the URL of the library publishes your form to that library.

3. Ensure that the browser option is checked and that Form Library is selected, as shown in Figure 8.16. Click Next.

4. Select to either create a new form library or update an existing one, as shown in Figure 8.16; see Chapter 2 for the scenario of creating a form library from InfoPath. Click Next.

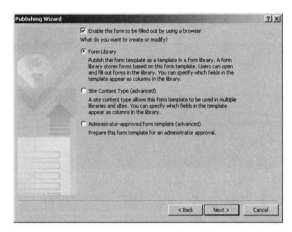

FIGURE 8.15
Enabling the form to be filled out by the browser allows it to be rendered in SharePoint.

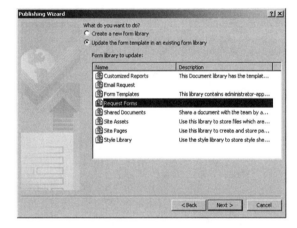

FIGURE 8.16
Updating the form template of the library replaces the default form with your form.

5. Select any fields to promote to the SharePoint library or used in a web part, as shown in Figure 8.18. (These will be explained in later sections/chapters.) Click Next.

6. Verify the information and click Publish. Your form is published to the form library you selected.

7. Check the Open This Form Library check box and click Close

8. Click Add Document to test your form in the browser, as shown in Figure 8.18.

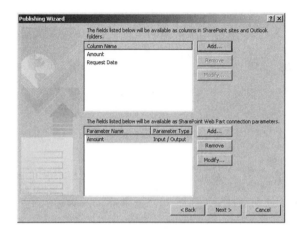

FIGURE 8.17
Selecting fields promotes them as properties for external SharePoint use.

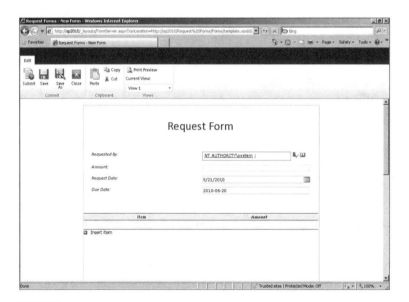

FIGURE 8.18
Publishing your form to the library renders your form in the browser.

Use Multiple Forms in SharePoint Libraries

Scenario/Problem: You need to provide several different forms from one SharePoint library.

Solution: Publish your form to SharePoint as a content type.

When you publish a form to a SharePoint library, there is a one-to-one relationship, and you can only use that form with that library. Publishing your forms as content types allows you to use them throughout your SharePoint site as well as use multiple forms in one SharePoint library.

To publish your form as a content type, follow these steps:

1. From File, Publish, click the SharePoint Server button.

2. In the Publishing Wizard, enter the location of the SharePoint site. Click Next.

3. Ensure that the browser option is checked and select the Site Content Type option, as shown in Figure 8.19. Click Next.

4. Select Create a New Content Type, as shown in Figure 8.20. Click Next.

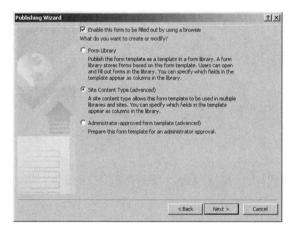

FIGURE 8.19
Selecting Site Content Type publishes your form as a content type in your SharePoint site.

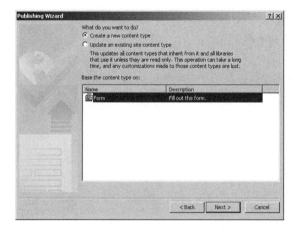

FIGURE 8.20
Selecting Create a New Content Type allows you to configure the content type details.

5. Enter a name and description for the content type. Click Next.

6. Enter a location and name within a URL path to save the form template on your SharePoint server, as shown in Figure 8.21. This is usually the form templates folder in your site collection (under the URL of FormServerTemplates). Click Next.

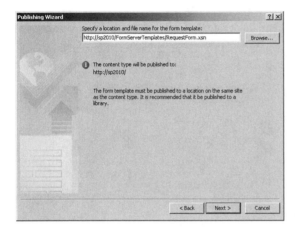

FIGURE 8.21
Entering the URL path determines where the form template will be saved.

NOTE Even though you are publishing your form as a content type, the form needs to be stored in SharePoint so that Forms Services can render new instances using the content type.

7. Click Next on the property promotion screen.

8. Click Publish. The form is published as a content type to your SharePoint site.

9. Click Close on the confirmation screen.

TIP If you promote fields as columns in your content type, those columns will be added to your library when you add the content type to that library.

10. Navigate to a form library in SharePoint where you want to associate the form.

11. On the Library ribbon bar, select Library Settings.

12. On the Library Settings page, click Advanced Settings.

13. Switch the Allow Management of Content Types option to Yes, as shown in Figure 8.22.

14. Optionally, click No on the Make "New Folder" Command Available option. Click OK.

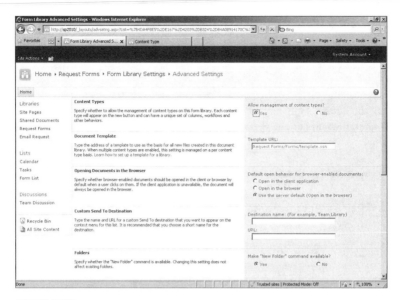

FIGURE 8.22
Switching the option to Yes allows you to add content types to the library.

15. Back on the Library Settings page, scroll down to the Content Types section and click the Add from Existing Site Content Types link.

16. Find and select the content type you published and click Add, as shown in Figure 8.23. Click OK.

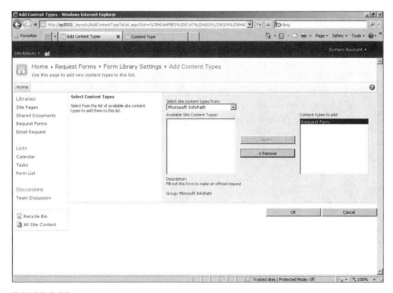

FIGURE 8.23
Adding a content type associates it with the SharePoint library.

> **TIP** Notice the description is the one you entered when creating the content type.

17. Back on the Library Settings page, scroll down to the Content Types section and click Change New Button Order and Default Content Type.

18. Uncheck the default form content type as Visible and change your new content type to be in the number one position from the top, as shown in Figure 8.24. Click OK.

FIGURE 8.24
Switching your content type to the top makes it the default content type.

19. Navigate back to the library and select the Documents ribbon bar.

20. The New Document menu now contains your content type, as shown in Figure 8.25, using the name and description you entered during the publishing process.

21. Repeat steps 1-20 for additional forms.

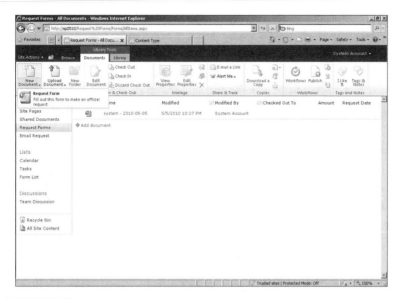

FIGURE 8.25
Clicking the New Document drop-down displays the available content types for your library.

Configure Web Service Submission

Scenario/Problem: You need your form to be submitted to a web service.

Solution: Click Submit Options and configure the web service settings.

Continuing from the enable form submission scenario, after you allow users to submit your form, the Send Form to a Single Destination option becomes enabled. Change the setting to Web Service, as shown in Figure 8.26.

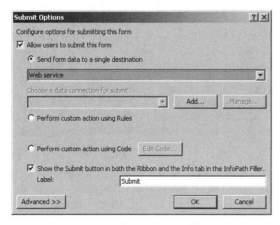

FIGURE 8.26
Selecting the Web Service option configures the form to submit to a web service.

Select a data connection that has been configured to a web service. If your form doesn't have one yet, you will need to configure a new web service connection.

> **TIP** Quickly get to the web service connection settings by clicking the To Other Locations button and selecting To Web Service on the ribbon bar instead of Submit Options.

To configure the web service connection, follow these steps:

1. Click the Add button on the Submit Options dialog. The Data Connection Wizard for the web service appears, as shown in Figure 8.27.

2. Enter the web service URL and click Next.

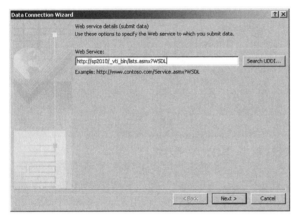

FIGURE 8.27
Entering the web service URL accesses the web methods available for submission.

> **TIP** Use the SharePoint web services to automate operations from your form without using code!

3. Select the desired web method, as shown in Figure 8.28. Click Next.

4. For each parameter of the web method, configure a mapping to a form field, as shown in Figure 8.29. Click Next.

> **TIP** Because most web methods need parameters, it is a good idea to figure out what parameters are needed ahead of time and at least create those fields on your form first. This makes the web service connection creation a bit easier.

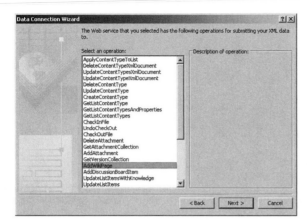

FIGURE 8.28
Selecting the web method allows you to submit form fields to that method.

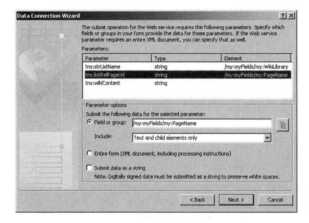

FIGURE 8.29
Mapping the fields to the web method parameters submits those values to the web service.

5. Enter a name for the connection and click Finish.

6. Back on the Submit Options dialog, ensure the web service connection is selected. Click OK.

Configure SharePoint Server Connection Submission

Scenario/Problem: You need your form to be submitted to an existing data connection in SharePoint.

Solution: Click Submit Options and configure the data connection settings.

Continuing from the enable form submission scenario, after you allow users to submit your form, the Send Form to a Single Destination option becomes enabled. Change the setting to Connection from a Data Connection Library, as shown in Figure 8.30.

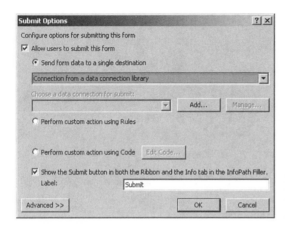

FIGURE 8.30
Selecting the Data Connection Library option configures the form to submit using an existing connection on your SharePoint site.

Select a data connection that has been configured to a data connection file on your SharePoint site. If your form doesn't have one yet, you will need to configure a new SharePoint Server connection to the data connection file.

> **TIP** Quickly get to the SharePoint data connection settings by clicking the To Other Locations button and selecting To SharePoint Server Connection on the ribbon bar instead of Submit Options.

To configure the SharePoint Server connection, follow these steps:

1. Click the Add button on the Submit Options dialog. The Data Connection Wizard for the SharePoint Server connection appears, as shown in Figure 8.31.

2. Click Manage Sites. The Manage Sites dialog appears, which displays the current sites available to use for a data connection, as shown in Figure 8.32.

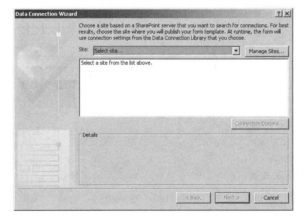

FIGURE 8.31
Selecting a site determines where to look for the data connection file.

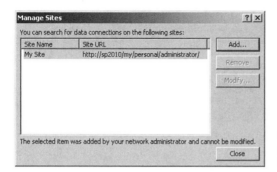

FIGURE 8.32
Adding sites to the managed sites list allows them to be selected.

3. Click Add and enter your main SharePoint site and display name, as shown in Figure 8.33. Click OK. Your site appears in the managed list. Click Close.

FIGURE 8.33
Entering a URL and display name enters the site into the managed sites list.

TIP Make sure your site has a data connections library with at least one data connection file. See Chapter 9, "Using Data in SharePoint Forms," for instructions on creating a data connection file.

4. Back on the Data Connection Wizard dialog, select the managed site that you entered and select the data connection file. Click Next.

5. Depending on the type of data connection, you may need to configure the related settings. Click Next.

6. Click Finish to generate the submit connection against the SharePoint Server connection file.

Modify the Available Menu Buttons During Form Submission

Scenario/Problem: You need to control which menu buttons display when the user is filling out your form.

Solution: Modify the web browser form options to hide or show the available menu items.

The web browser form options allow you to control which menu commands are available to users while they are filing out the form. For example, when using the submit options in your form (that is, you want the user to submit the form and not save it), you might not want to have the Save or Save As options available to your user.

The menu buttons either appear on the toolbar or ribbon bar depending on how your form is rendered in the browser. You may control where the toolbar appears if the ribbon bar is not available.

Here are the steps to access and modify the web browser form options:

1. Select File, Info and click the Form Options button, as shown in Figure 8.34.

2. Select the Web Browser category, as shown in Figure 8.35.

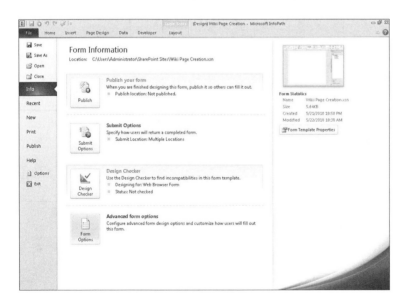

FIGURE 8.34
Clicking Form Options allows you to modify various settings specific to your form.

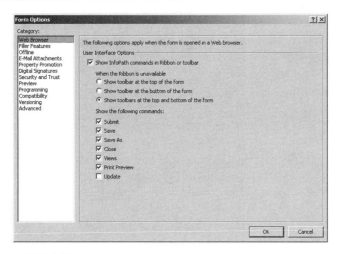

FIGURE 8.35
Modifying the web browser options determines which commands are available.

3. Modify the settings accordingly. Click OK.

TIP You may uncheck the Show InfoPath Commands option to completely hide all commands, but do this only if you have other buttons or controls that handle the submission or saving of your form.

CHAPTER 9

Using Data in SharePoint Forms

This chapter explores the data integration points within InfoPath and explains how to utilize business data within your form controls and fields.

One of the most compelling aspects of InfoPath with SharePoint 2010 is the ability to access and use business data from various sources. Whether it's to populate drop-downs or display information, InfoPath has the ability to integrate with data sources and bind fields or controls to the data elements.

Instead of hard-coding values in your form, accessing centralized business data allows you to dynamically populate options and selections without having to continually update and republish your forms.

Use Data From a Database

Scenario/Problem: You need to use data from a SQL Server database in your form.

Solution: Create a data connection to the SQL Server database.

InfoPath can access data from a SQL Server database, allowing you to capitalize on existing business data that may be stored in a central repository or data warehouse. Accessing the database information requires several steps, including creating a local data link file, the initial InfoPath connection, and the SharePoint Server data connection such that your form can access the data when rendered in SharePoint.So let's start with the first task, which is to create a local data link file.

To create a local data link file, follow these steps:

1. On your desktop, right-click and select New, Text Document.

2. Rename the text document to SQL Server.udl and click Yes on the warning about changing the file extension. Your file should look similar to Figure 9.1.

3. Double-click the file to open the connection properties.

4. On the Data Link Properties connection tab, select the database server from the drop-down, enter the database credentials, and select the database, as shown in Figure 9.2. Select the Allow Saving Password option if you are using SQL Server authentication. Click OK.

NOTE   You might have issues using Windows Authentication if the database server is not part of the SharePoint farm. The easier, streamlined option is to use SQL Server authentication with an account that has read privileges to the database you need to access. The password will ultimately be stored in the connection file in SharePoint. Securing the data connections library is one way to keep it hidden.

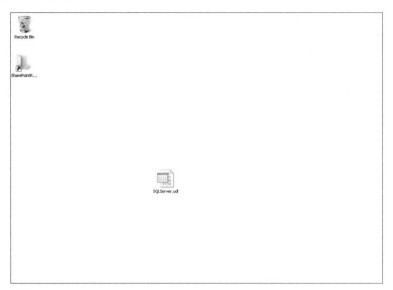

FIGURE 9.1
Creating a local UDL file allows you to create the initial SQL Server connection.

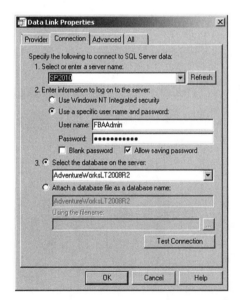

FIGURE 9.2
Configuring the connection creates the local data link file for your SQL Server database.

Now that the data link file is created, you need to configure the InfoPath connection using that file. To do this, follow these steps:

1. In InfoPath Designer, select the Data ribbon bar. Click the From Other Sources button and select From Database, as shown in Figure 9.3.

2. In the Data Connection Wizard dialog, click the Select Database button and navigate to the data link file you created in the previous steps, as shown in Figure 9.4. Click Open.

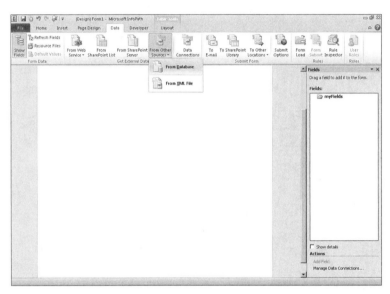

FIGURE 9.3
Clicking the Database button allows you to create the appropriate data connection.

FIGURE 9.4
Selecting the data link file allows you to configure the database connection.

3. Select a table from the database where you need to retrieve data, as shown in Figure 9.5. Click OK.

4. Unselect any columns that you don't need back in the wizard dialog, as shown in Figure 9.6.

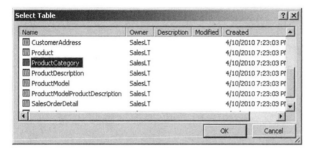

FIGURE 9.5
Selecting a table determines where the data will come from.

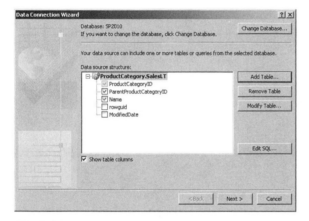

FIGURE 9.6
Selecting the columns determines which data elements are retrieved.

5. You may add additional tables by clicking the Add Table button and selecting another table, as shown in Figure 9.7, and clicking Next.

6. Remove any relationships that are not applicable, such as Name and Modified Date, as shown in Figure 9.8. Click Finish.

TIP In this example, only the ProductCategoryID matches between the two tables. If you leave the other relationships, no data will be returned from the Product table.

FIGURE 9.7

Adding additional tables allows you to access more data from the same connection.

FIGURE 9.8

Selecting only the foreign key columns designates a relationship between the added tables.

7. Back on the Data Connection Wizard dialog, click Next.

8. You may optionally store a copy of the data in the form by checking the check box. Click Next.

9. Enter a name for the data connection, as shown in Figure 9.9. If you are using the data for a selection that is needed when the form is opened, leave the Automatically Retrieve Data option checked. Otherwise, you may uncheck it for quicker performance. Click Finish.

The data connection is now available inside InfoPath. It will work locally, but when deployed to SharePoint, you could experience data access issues. This may be because of authentication or other access issues. To use the database connection in SharePoint successfully, it is recommended that you convert this connection to a centralized data connection file. The next section explains this process.

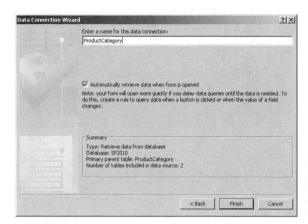

FIGURE 9.9
Entering a name for the connection stores the connection in InfoPath using that name.

Convert an InfoPath Connection to a SharePoint Connection File

Scenario/Problem: You need to access your data connections from within SharePoint.

Solution: Select the data connection and click the Convert to Connection File button.

Although this scenario is an extension of the previous scenario, the steps are the same for any type of data connection within InfoPath. To convert an InfoPath connection to a file in SharePoint, follow these steps:

1. Select the Data ribbon bar and select Data Connections.

2. Select the data connection you want to convert and click the Convert to Connection File button, as shown in Figure 9.10.

3. Enter the path and filename, as shown in Figure 9.11. Click OK.

TIP Leaving the connection relative to the site collection means that you may publish your form to a different environment, and InfoPath will look in the same data connection library for the same file. For example, if your production environment contains the connection file at http://prodsp2010/data connections/productcategory. udcx, based on this scenario, you do not need to change anything in your form.

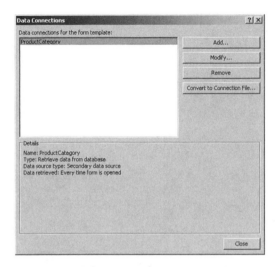

FIGURE 9.10
Selecting an InfoPath connection allows you to convert it to a connection file.

FIGURE 9.11
Entering the full path and filename saves the connection file in the specified location.

4. Navigate to your data connections library in SharePoint and select Approve/ Reject from the item menu, as shown in Figure 9.12.

5. Select the Approved option, as shown in Figure 9.13. Click OK.

TIP Saving a new connection in the SharePoint sets the approval status to Pending. You may not be able to use the connection or access data until the connection file has been approved.

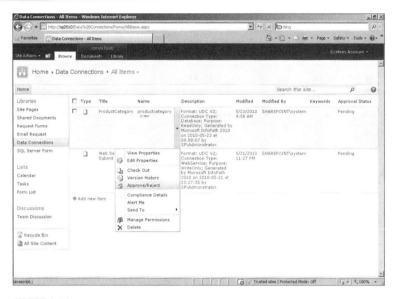

FIGURE 9.12
Selecting Approve/Reject allows you to change the approval status of the data connection.

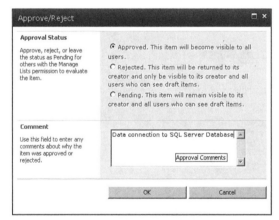

FIGURE 9.13
Approving the data connection file allows it to be used within SharePoint.

Use Data From a SharePoint List

Scenario/Problem: You need to use data that is stored within an existing SharePoint list.

Solution: Create a data connection to the SharePoint list.

A common data source for SharePoint forms is a SharePoint list. If the list contains business entities and is the main repository for those items, it only makes sense to leverage them within you form if needed.

To access data from a SharePoint list in your form, follow these steps:

1. In InfoPath Designer, select the Data ribbon bar. Click the From SharePoint List button, as shown in Figure 9.14. The Data Connection Wizard appears.

2. In the Data Connection Wizard dialog, enter the URL the SharePoint site that contains the list you need to access, as shown in Figure 9.15. Click Next.

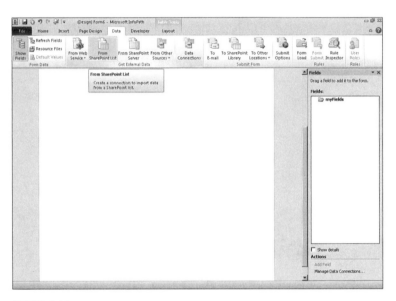

FIGURE 9.14
Clicking the From SharePoint List button allows you to create the appropriate data connection.

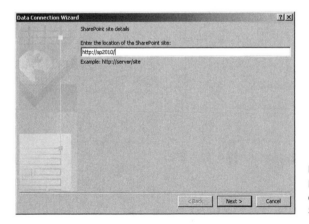

FIGURE 9.15
Entering the SharePoint site determines where to find the SharePoint list.

3. Select the SharePoint list from the available lists as shown in Figure 9.16. Click Next.

4. Select the fields you would like to use in your form from the list and how the items should be sorted, as shown in Figure 9.17. Click Next.

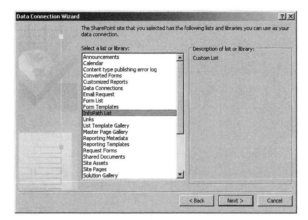

FIGURE 9.16
Selecting the list creates the connection for that list's data.

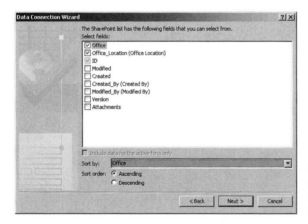

FIGURE 9.17
Selecting the list fields determines what item elements are retrieved.

TIP   If the display name is different from the underlying list column name, you will see the display name in parentheses.

5. Click Next on the Store a Copy screen.

6. Provide a connection name and click Finish.

Use Data From a SharePoint Data Connection File

Scenario/Problem: You need to use data in your form from a data connection file in SharePoint.

Solution: Create an InfoPath data connection to the SharePoint data connection file.

Once you begin creating connections and converting them to SharePoint data connection files, chances are you will have forms that need similar information (such as for standard business selections in drop-down controls) and therefore need to use a data connection file that you have already created previously.

TIP Don't reinvent the wheel! Use already created SharePoint data connection files to streamline form creation.

The whole idea of creating SharePoint connection files is for this purpose so let's connect a new form to an existing SharePoint data connection file:

1. In InfoPath Designer, select the Data ribbon bar. Click the From SharePoint Server button, as shown in Figure 9.18. The Data Connection Wizard appears.

2. In the Data Connection Wizard dialog, select the site from the drop-down, expand the Data Connections item, and select the desired data connection file, as shown Figure 9.19. Click Next.

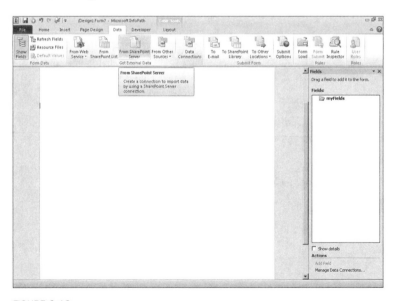

FIGURE 9.18
Clicking the From SharePoint Server button allows you leverage existing data connections in SharePoint.

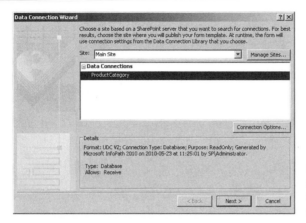

FIGURE 9.19
Selecting the data connection determines which SharePoint data connection file to use.

TIP If your site doesn't appear in the drop-down, use the Manage Sites to add it to the list. See Chapter 8, "Submitting and Publishing in SharePoint," for more details on adding a new managed site.

3. Click Next on the Store a Copy screen.

4. Provide a connection name and click Finish.

Use Data from a (SOAP) Web Service

Scenario/Problem: You need to use data that is returned from a web service.

Solution: Create a data connection to the web service.

Many times an organization may isolate data layers by providing access to web services instead of directly to the database. To access data from a SOAP-based web service in your form, follow these steps:

1. In InfoPath Designer, select the Data ribbon bar. Click the From Web Service button and select From SOAP Web Service, as shown in Figure 9.20. The Data Connection Wizard appears.

2. In the Data Connection Wizard dialog, enter the URL of the web service along with the ?WSDL suffix, as shown in Figure 9.21. Click Next.

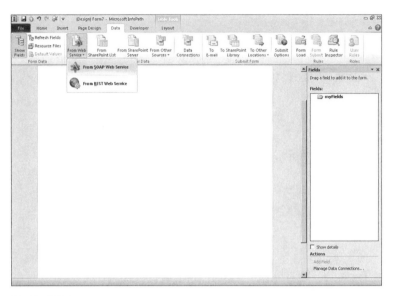

FIGURE 9.20
Selecting the From SOAP Web Service allows you to create the appropriate data connection.

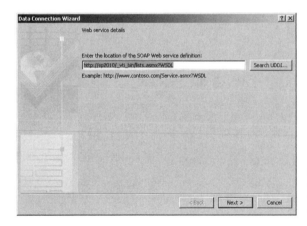

FIGURE 9.21
Entering the web service
URL accesses the available
methods for data retrieval.

3. Select the web method you want to use to retrieve information, as shown in
   Figure 9.22. Click Next.

NOTE   In this example, we are using a SharePoint system web service. This is
solely for example purposes. It is probably easier to get list items from a SharePoint
List connection than through the web service.

4. Enter sample values for the web service parameters so that InfoPath can understand what data to expect, as shown in Figure 9.23. Click Next.

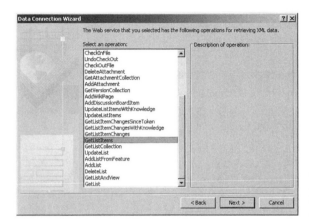

FIGURE 9.22
Selecting the web method determines where the data will be coming from.

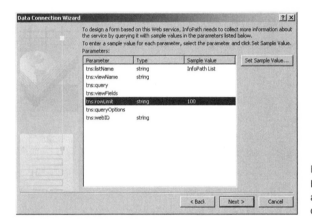

FIGURE 9.23
Entering sample values assists in determining what data to expect.

5. Click Next on the Store a Copy screen.

6. Provide a connection name and click Finish.

NOTE The SharePoint web services are being shown here for example purposes and may not execute if all values are not provided.

Populate a Drop-Down List with Data

Scenario/Problem: You need to provide users a selection option based on a data source.

Solution: Configure the control to get choices from an external data source.

Populating a drop-down list (or any other list-based control) is probably one of the most common uses of external business data in SharePoint forms. Once a data connection has been established on your form, using the data in a drop-down list is just a few clicks away.

For this scenario, let's use the SQL Server connection that we created in a previous scenario of this chapter. The first table was the ProductCategory, so let's hook that up:

1. Drag a drop-down list control onto your form.

2. Right-click the control and select the Drop-Down List Box Properties.

3. Rename the field to ProductCategory and change the data type to Whole Number (Integer).

4. In the List Box choices, select Get Choices from an External Data Source.

5. In the Data Source drop-down, select the data source (ProductCategory in this example). The Value and Display Name entries default to ProductCategoryID, as shown in Figure 9.24.

TIP Typically, you want the Value of the selection to be the unique identifier column in the database and to use the name or description field as the Display Name.

6. In the Display Name field, click the Field button and change the field to Name field, as shown in Figure 9.25. This is the field that is displayed to the user in the drop-down.

7. Click OK to save the property changes.

TIP Use the same configuration steps for other list-based controls, such as a list box.

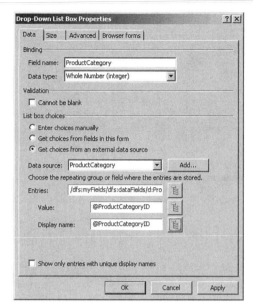

FIGURE 9.24
Selecting the data source determines which fields are available to bind to the control.

FIGURE 9.25
Configuring the display name determines which data element is displayed to the user.

Preview your form to test the drop-down population. An example is shown in Figure 9.26.

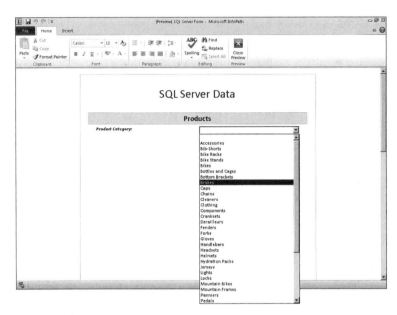

FIGURE 9.26
Previewing your form shows that the drop-down is being populated with the configured data.

Populate a Drop-Down List with Data Based on Another Selection (Cascading Drop-Down)

Scenario/Problem: You need to present the user with options in a drop-down based on a previous selection.

Solution: Filter the data that is displayed in the dependent drop-down list.

When the available selections in one drop-down list are dependent on previous selections in another drop-down list, these are called "cascading drop-downs." The values available in the dependent control are filtered by some aspect of the other control's selection.

TIP Use the same concept for other controls and/or data sources.

Continuing with the previous scenario and our established SQL Server data connection, let's add a Product drop-down list to the form that presents the available products based on the Product Category selection, as shown in Figure 9.27. This is the dependent drop-down list.

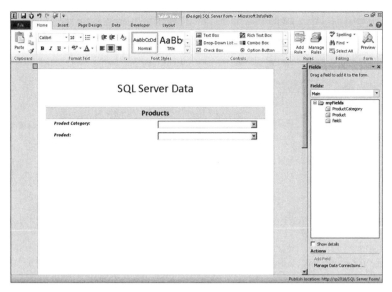

FIGURE 9.27
Adding another drop-down list control allows you to make it dependent.

To configure the data source and the dependency on Product Category, follow these steps:

1. Right-click the dependent drop-down and select the Drop-Down List Box Properties.

2. Name the drop-down control Product and change the data type to Whole Number (Integer).

3. In the List Box choices, select Get Choices from an External Data Source.

4. In the Data Source drop-down, select the data source (ProductCategory in this example).

5. Click the Fields button next to the Entries (the ToolTip states Select XPath). The Select Field or Group dialog appears.

6. Select the Product group, as shown in Figure 9.28, to use data from the Product table.

> **NOTE** This example assumes that you added the Product table along with Product Category when creating the SQL Server data connection. You may also use a separate data connection for the Product table as long as the foreign key of ProductCategoryID matches the values in the Product Category table.

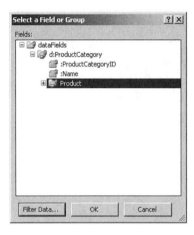

FIGURE 9.28

Selecting the Product group allows you to use data from the Product table.

1. Click the Filter button, and on the Filter Data dialog, click the Add button.

2. In the first drop-down, select Select a Field or Group option and select ProductCategoryID from the Product grouping, as shown in Figure 9.29 to ensure the dependency filters on the product category. Click OK.

FIGURE 9.29

Selecting the ProductCategoryID from Products ensures the dependency filters on the product category

3. In the last drop-down, select the Select a Field or Group option and select your ProductCategory field from the Main data connection, as shown in Figure 9.30, to connect the dependency to the ProductCategory selection. (You may need to change the data source at the top of the dialog.) Click OK.

   The filter condition, which is the basis of the drop-down dependency, should look similar to Figure 9.31. Click OK.

4. Click OK on the Filter Data dialog.

5. Click OK on the Select a Field or Group dialog.

6. Click the Fields button next to the Value entry and select ProductID from the Product group.

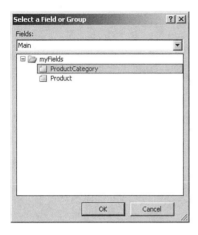

FIGURE 9.30

Selecting the ProductCategory field from makes the Product list dependent on that selection.

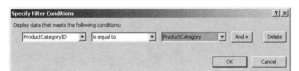

FIGURE 9.31

Creating the filter condition provides the basis of the dependency between the drop-down lists.

7. Click the Fields button next to the Display Name entry and select the Name from the Product group. Your properties screen should look similar to Figure 9.32. Click OK.

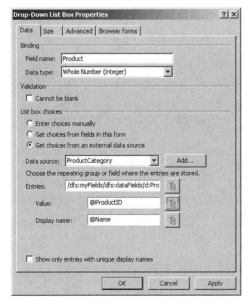

FIGURE 9.32

Selecting the product fields allows the drop-down to be populated with the filtered product data.

Previewing your form shows that the available products in the drop-down are dependent on the product category that is selected as shown in Figure 9.33.

If you select a product category and product but then change the product category, you may notice that a number appears in the product drop-down. This is the ID of the previous selection. Because the product category changes, so does the list of available products, and therefore the previous selection is no longer a valid selection in the list.

FIGURE 9.33
Selecting a product category determines which products appear in the products drop-down list.

To clear this up, add a rule on the product category such that when that value changes, you clear the selected product. Here are the steps:

1. Select the Product Category drop-down.

2. Click the Add Rule button from the ribbon bar and select This Field Changes, Set a Field's Value, as shown in Figure 9.34, to set the condition of the rule.

3. On the Rule Details dialog, click the Fields button and select the Product field from the Main data source, as shown in Figure 9.35, and leave the Value blank to clear the selected product. Click OK.

Now anytime the product category is changed, the product selection is cleared. This resolves the phantom number issue.

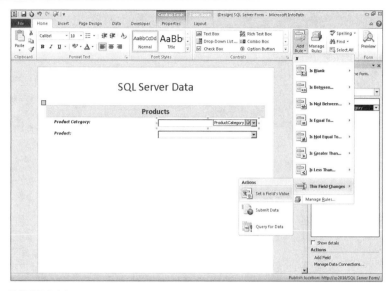

FIGURE 9.34
Selecting the Add Rule items sets the condition of the rule.

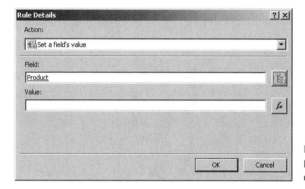

FIGURE 9.35
Leaving the Value entry blank clears the Product field.

Display Data from a SharePoint List

Scenario/Problem: You need to present the user with options based on data in a SharePoint list.

Solution: Configure a control to use the SharePoint list data.

In this scenario, we use SharePoint list data to display options to the user and to display additional information from the list. For example purposes, we use a list of offices, as shown in Figure 9.36, because this is a central location that stores business data and helps leverage form options.

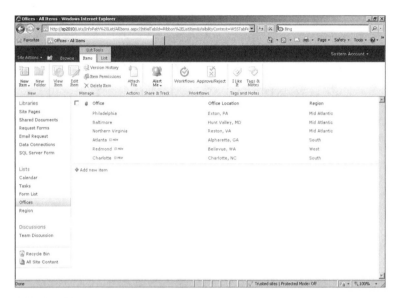

FIGURE 9.36
Using a central list that stores business data helps leverage form options.

Leveraging the data in this list is accomplished by completing the following steps:

1. Configure a SharePoint List data connection to your list, as explained in previous scenarios of this chapter.

2. Drag a drop-down list onto your form and name the field Office.

3. Drag a text box onto your form and name the field OfficeLocation. (This is another column in the same list.)

4. Right-click the Office drop-down list, and select the Drop-down List Box properties.

5. Choose the Get Choices from an External Data Source, option and select the SharePoint List data connection from the Data Source drop-down.

6. Select the Value and Display Name fields, as shown in Figure 9.37, using the list item ID to uniquely identify each entry. Click OK.

> **TIP** It is a good idea to preview your form midway through to make sure things are hooked up and working correctly.

7. Right-click the OfficeLocation text box and select Text Box Properties.

8. Click the Function button next to the Value entry.

9. Click the Insert Field or Group button on the Insert Formula dialog.

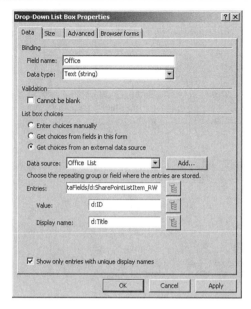

FIGURE 9.37
The internal list item ID uniquely identifies each list entry.

10. Select the Office Location list column, as shown in Figure 9.38, to set the text box to display the location value. (You may need to switch the data source selection to the SharePoint List data connection.)

FIGURE 9.38
Selecting another list column sets the text box to display that value.

11. Click the Filter Data button and add a Filter condition such that the ID in the SharePoint List is equal to the value of the selected Office on your form, as shown in Figure 9.39. This determines which location value is shown in the text box. Click OK.

12. Click OK on the Filter Data dialog.

13. Click OK on the Select a Field or Group dialog. The formula for the default value is generated from the filter condition, as shown in Figure 9.40. Click OK.

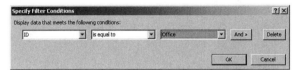

FIGURE 9.39
Filtering the list data determines which location is shown in the text box.

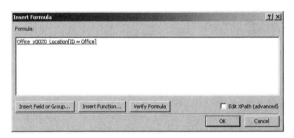

FIGURE 9.40
Creating the filter condition generates the formula for the default value.

14. Click OK on the Text Box properties dialog.

15. Previewing your form enables you to select a value from the list and have another value from the same list item display in the text box, as shown in Figure 9.41.

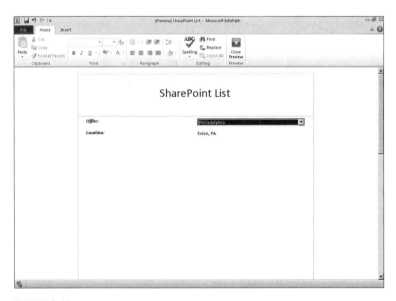

FIGURE 9.41
Selecting a value from the list populates the text box with another value from the same list item.

> **TIP** Change the text box properties to read-only and remove the borders/shading to use it for display-only purposes as implemented in this example.

Display a Repeating Table From a SharePoint List

Scenario/Problem: You need to display multiple values from a SharePoint list.

Solution: Drag the SharePointListItem_RW group from the SharePoint List data connection onto your form and select Repeating Table.

That's the easy answer but we want to expand on that simple instruction. The Office list that we used in the previous scenario has a Region column which is actually a lookup to another list. There is a Region list that contains the available regions in which the offices exist. Therefore, only the list item ID of the Region list item is stored in the Region column of the Office list. (We will uncover this in a moment.)

For educational purposes, let's drag the list group from the SharePoint List data connection onto the form and select Repeating Table, as shown in Figure 9.42.

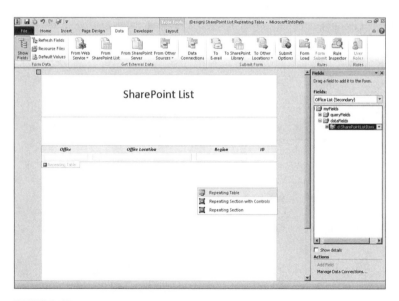

FIGURE 9.42
Dragging a group from a data source onto your form allows you to generate a repeating table.

Previewing the form at this stage explains the Region relationship in which only the ID of the Region is stored, as shown in Figure 9.43; the stored values are uncovered.

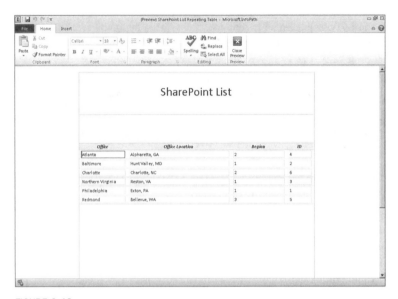

FIGURE 9.43
Displaying the list items uncovers the stored values.

Let's enhance the form and connect a region selection for the table. First we need to setup the Region selection.

To setup the Region selection, follow these steps:

1. Create a data connection to the Region SharePoint list.

2. Remove the Region and ID columns from the repeating table on the form.

3. Drag a list box control (or any list box-based control) onto your form and name the field Region.

4. Connect the list box control to the Region SharePoint list data connection using the list ID column for the Value and the Title column for the Display Name. Your form should look similar to Figure 9.44 after following these steps.

Now we need to filter the repeating table data based on the region selection:

1. Select the Region list box control.

2. Click Add Rule and select This Field Changes, Set a Field's Value, as shown in Figure 9.45, to create the condition of the data rule which will filter the Office list data.

> **TIP** The best practice is to always filter data (if possible) when displaying multiple rows at one time, especially from a SharePoint list.

3. In the Rule Details dialog, click the Fields button next to the Field entry.

4. Change the data source to the Office List connection.

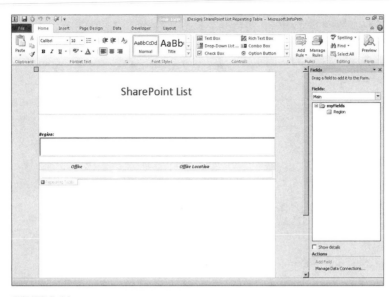

FIGURE 9.44
After following the steps, your form should look like this.

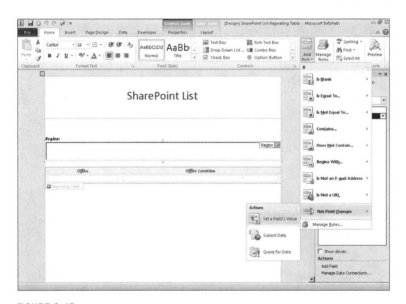

FIGURE 9.45
Adding a rule allows you to filter the Office list data.

5. Expand the queryFields group and the SharePointListItem_RW group. Select the Region field, as shown in Figure 9.46, to set the field's value. Click OK.

FIGURE 9.46
Selecting the Region field allows you to set that field's value.

6. Click the Function button next to the Value entry.

7. Click the Insert Field or Group button.

8. Select the Region field from your main data source to use the selected value of the region list box, as shown in Figure 4.47. Click OK.

FIGURE 9.47
Selecting the form's Region field allows you to use the selected value of the list box.

9. Click OK on the Insert Formula dialog. The formula is a period (.) because we are referencing the value of the current control. We are adding the rule on the Region list box and setting the query value to the value of the selected region, so your Rules Detail should look similar to Figure 9.48.

10. Click OK. The Rules pane appears on the screen. We are already setting the query field value in the rule, but we need to query the data to retrieve the proper SharePoint list items.

11. In the Rules pane, select Add, Query for Data, as shown in Figure 9.49, to add another action to the rule. The Rule Details dialog appears again.

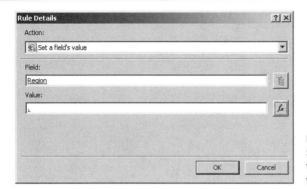

FIGURE 9.48
Specifying the rule details sets the Region query field to the value of the selected Region.

FIGURE 9.49
Clicking Add and selecting an action adds another action to the rule.

12. In the Rule Details dialog, ensure that the Office List data connection is selected, as shown in Figure 9.50. Click OK to create the action for querying against the SharePoint list.

13. Preview the form to test the rule. Selecting a region from the list box changes (or filters) the list items in the table, only showing the offices in the selected region, as demonstrated in Figure 9.51.

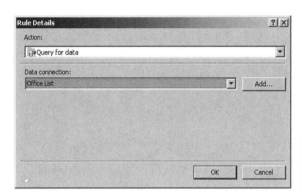

FIGURE 9.50
Selecting the Office List data connection queries the SharePoint list.

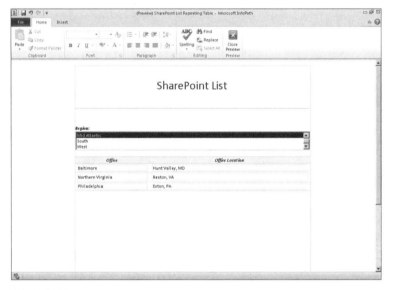

FIGURE 9.51
Selecting a region filters the items shown in the table.

> **TIP** Don't want anything to show in the table until a region is selected? Modify the SharePoint list data connection (Data ribbon bar, Data Connections button) and uncheck the Automatically Retrieve Data When Form Is Opened option.

Leverage External Data from a SharePoint External

Scenario/Problem: You need to allow the user to select an entity from an external content type.

Solution: Use the external item picker and configure to use the SharePoint external content type.

Content Type (Business Data Connectivity Services)

External content types (ECT) are managed by SharePoint using the Business Data Connectivity Services (BCS) application. They may be generated by using Visual Studio 2010, SharePoint Designer 2010, or from an application definition file.

To leverage external data from BCS in your form, follow these steps:

1. Drag an external item picker control onto your form.

2. Right-click the control and select External Item Picker Properties.

3. Click the General tab and enter the ECT values to access the external data, as shown in Figure 9.52. Here are explanations of the required fields:

   ECT Namespace: The main SharePoint root that contains the external content type.

   ECT Name: The name of the external content type

   System Instance Name: The actual back-end system name or database name

   Finder Name: The name of the method that returns all items (in SharePoint 2010, usually the ReadList() method)

   Display Field Name: The external content type field name to display to the user

   Dialog Title: The title of the Picker dialog that is shown to the user when they are selecting an external item

TIP Use SharePoint Designer 2010 or Central Administration to assist in finding the values of the external content type.

4. Click the Other Settings tab.

5. Under Default , you may optionally enter a default search term. If this is left blank, all values will be returned when the Picker dialog appears.

6. Change the Picker Mode option to Connect to External Data Source Through SharePoint, as shown in Figure 9.53, such that the external data connection is handled through SharePoint.

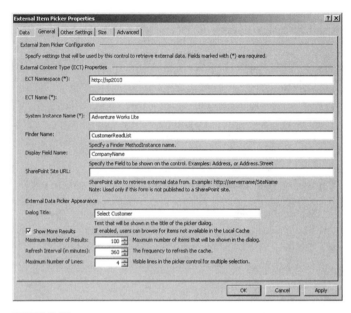

FIGURE 9.52
Entering the ECT values allows you to access the external data.

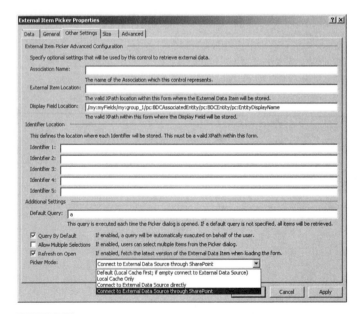

FIGURE 9.53
Changing the Picker Mode allows your form to connect to external data through SharePoint.

4. Click OK to save the external item picker properties.

5. Publish the form to SharePoint to test. Preview mode won't work because you are connecting to the external content type through SharePoint.

6. Click the Select External Item(s) button to confirm that a user can select an item from the external content type

NOTE   The search items and display field in the Picker dialog depend on how the external content type was created and which filters were implemented on the finder method.

Leverage External Data from a REST Web Service

Scenario/Problem: You need to present users with data from a REST web service.

Solution: Configure the REST web service data connection and use rules to change the parameters.

REST web services return XML documents and take parameters through the URL query string. If you need the parameters to be dynamic, they may be changed by using rules. This scenario steps through these processes.

First let's create a connection to the REST web service:

1. In InfoPath Designer, select the Data ribbon bar. Click the From Web Service button and select From REST Web Service, as shown in Figure 9.54. The Data Connection Wizard appears.

2. In the Data Connection Wizard dialog, enter the URL of the web service along with the appropriate query parameters, as shown in Figure 9.56, to retrieve data based on the parameters.

NOTE   This example uses a public REST web service from NOAA that is available through the Internet. You may use the same one to follow along: http://www.weather.gov/forecasts/xml/sample_products/browser_interface/ndfdXMLclient.php?zipCodeList=19115&product=time-series&begin=2010-05-27T00:00:00&end=2010-05-28T00:00:00&maxt=maxt&mint=mint.

See http://www.weather.gov/forecasts/xml/rest.php for more information about available weather-based REST web services (or to copy and paste sample URLs into your form).

It is recommended to visit the site and grab the latest URL examples as these change, and you may experience difficulty entering the URL verbatim from this chapter.

3. Click Next. Enter a name for the data connection and click Finish.

4. From the Data ribbon bar, click the Show Fields button. The Fields Pane appears.

5. Switch the data source to the REST Web Service connection.

6. Drag the "data" group onto the form, as shown in Figure 9.55, to examine what data comes back from the web service.

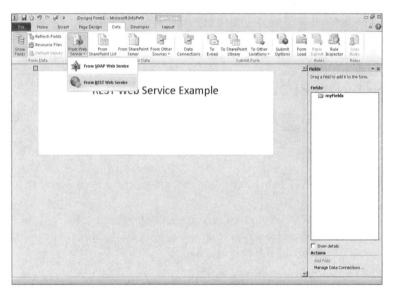

FIGURE 9.54
Selecting the From REST Web Service allows you to create the appropriate data connection.

7. Preview the form to retrieve and display the data from the web service, as shown in Figure 9.56.

It looks like we only need the temperature information, which is returning the high and the low for the day based on the passed-in ZIP code. Therefore, remove all the sections on the form and drag over the temperature group such that we display only the information we need on the form. Optionally, remove the Time, Units, and Time Layout columns from the repeating table.

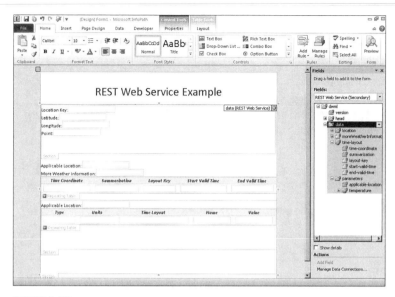

FIGURE 9.55
Placing the data group onto your form allows you to examine the returned data from the web service.

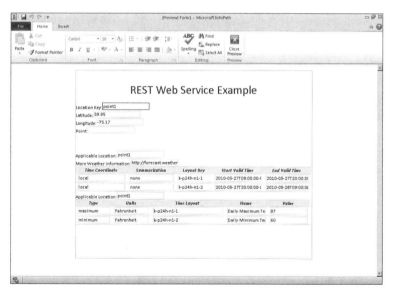

FIGURE 9.56
Previewing the form retrieves and displays the data from the web service.

Now let's add some dynamics to the web service call. To do this, follow these steps:

1. Drag a drop-down list box (or list-based) control onto your form. Name the field City.

2. Connect the list box to a data source or enter values for example purposes. Because the web service takes in a ZIP code, you need the Value of the list box to be a ZIP code and the Display Name to be a city name. Figure 9.57 demonstrates manually entered values for the list.

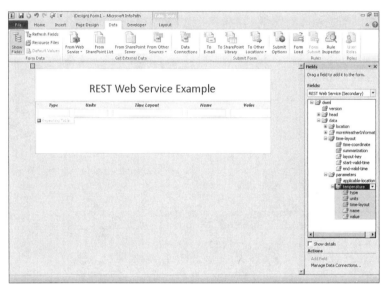

FIGURE 9.57
Entering manual entries allows the list box to be populated with available ZIP codes / cities.

3. Select the City drop-down list and click Add Rule, This Field Changes, Query for Data.

4. Select the REST Web Service on the Rule Details dialog and click OK. The Rules pane appears on the screen.

5. In the Rules Pane select Add and select Change REST URL, as shown in Figure 9.58, to add an action that changes the URL parameters to the rule. The Rule Details dialog appears.

6. In the Rule pane, click the Function button. The resultant value for the URL needs to be a string. Therefore, we'll use the concat function to construct a string using static text as well as the field value of City on the form.

7. Enter the concat function and use http://www.weather.gov/forecasts/xml/sample_products/browser_interface/ndfdXMLclient.php?zipCodeList= for the first value.

FIGURE 9.58

Adding a Change REST URL action allows the rule to change the URL parameters.

8. For the second value, click the Insert Field or Group button and select the City field from the main data source. Because the rule is on the City drop-down list, the field is represented as a period (.) in the formula.

9. Remove the hard-coded ZIP code from the text and use the remaining portion of the URL for the third value in the concat() function (&product=time-series&begin=2010-05-27T00:00:00&end=2010-05-28T00:00:00&maxt=maxt& mint=mint). Your formula should look similar to Figure 9.59. Essentially, we are constructing a URL string using form values in place of hard-coded entries.

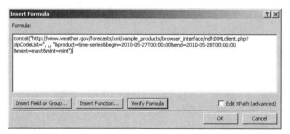

FIGURE 9.59

Using concat() constructs a URL string using form values.

TIP   Click Verify Formula to check your syntax!

> **TIP** Use the date functions to dynamically change the begin and end parameters in the URL example.

10. Click OK on the Insert Formula dialog.

11. Click OK on the Rule Details dialog.

12. In the Rules pane, click the drop-down menu on the Change REST URL action and select move up such that we change the URL first before querying the data source.

13. Preview the form to test the functionality. When the city is changed, the web service is queried and the new results are displayed.

> **TIP** Don't want anything to show in the table until a city is selected? Modify the REST web service data connection (Data ribbon bar, Data Connections button) and uncheck the Automatically Retrieve Data When Form Is Opened option.

CHAPTER 10

InfoPath Form Web Part

This chapter explores the use of the InfoPath Form web part, which is available in SharePoint 2010. The InfoPath Form web part enables you to display an InfoPath form designed for SharePoint. Because it is a web part, you may use it to connect and send data between other web parts.

Combining this functionality with list forms and list web parts opens the door for producing and providing extensive functionality within SharePoint. Use the concepts in this chapter to further expand your portal environment.

Add an InfoPath Form Web Part to a SharePoint Web Part Page

Scenario/Problem: You need to display an InfoPath form within a SharePoint web part page.

Solution: Edit the page, add the InfoPath Form web part, and configure.

To add and configure an InfoPath Form web part on a SharePoint web part page, follow these steps:

1. Navigate to the SharePoint page and select Edit Page from the ribbon bar. (Or create a new web part page.)

2. Click Add a Web Part in the zone where you want the InfoPath Form web part.

3. Select the Forms category and select InfoPath Form Web Part, as shown in Figure 10.1. Click Add to add it to the selected zone.

4. From the web part item menu, select Edit Web Part, as shown in Figure 10.2, to open the tool pane.

FIGURE 10.1
Selecting InfoPath Form Web Part allows you to add it to your page.

FIGURE 10.2
Editing the web part opens the tool pane.

5. In the web part tool pane, select the form library that contains the form you want to display. Make sure your form is selected in the Content Type drop-down, as shown in Figure 10.3.

> **TIP** Although it states that you may select only forms that have been published to a library or list, you may also select forms that have been published as content types and added to the library or list.

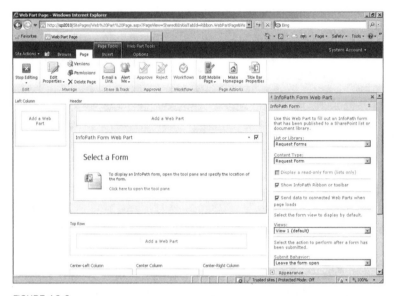

FIGURE 10.3
Selecting the library and content type configures the form to be displayed.

6. Click OK in the web part tool pane.

7. Click Stop Editing on the ribbon bar to save the page.

Browsing the page displays the InfoPath form on the page itself. Clicking the Edit tab in the ribbon bar displays the InfoPath commands to the user, as shown in Figure 10.4.

> **TIP** The same steps can be used for a wiki page. Simply select the Web Part button from the Insert ribbon bar menu for step 2.

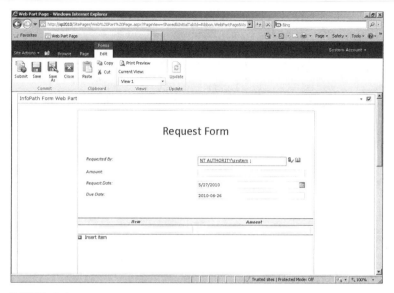

FIGURE 10.4
Clicking the Edit tab displays the InfoPath commands available for the form.

Create a Master/Detail Display Form for SharePoint Lists

Scenario/Problem: You have two lists that are related and want to show the details all on one page.

Solution: Edit the display form of the parent list and add the related list.

Revisiting the Office and Region lists from Chapter 9, "Using Data in SharePoint Forms," each Office entry has a region selection that is a lookup to the Region list. Therefore, you can modify the display form for the Region list such that the corresponding offices are shown on the same page.

To accomplish this, navigate to the parent list and follow these steps:

1. From the List ribbon bar select the Modify Form Web Parts button and select (Item) Display Form, as shown in Figure 10.5, to edit the display form page. The display form is presented in edit mode.

NOTE If you did not customize the form of the list, the drop-down will display only the default forms.

2. From the Insert ribbon bar, select Related List and click the related list to insert the details onto the display form page, as shown in Figure 10.6.

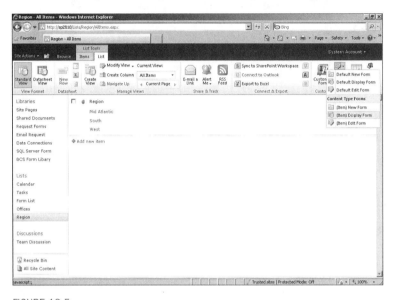

FIGURE 10.5
Clicking Modify Form Web Parts allows you to edit the form pages.

FIGURE 10.6
Inserting a related list adds the details to the display form page.

3. On the Page ribbon bar, click Stop Editing to save your changes.

4. Back in the Regions list, clicking a region opens the display form and shows the related offices, as shown in Figure 10.7.

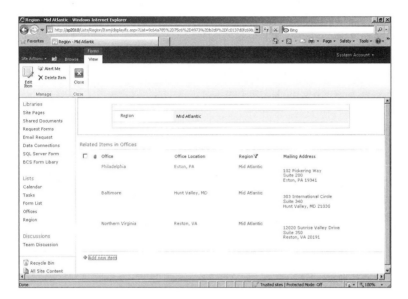

FIGURE 10.7
Viewing a region item displays the related offices.

TIP If you don't want the lookup column to be displayed (because it shows the same entry for each item), you can create a new view in the related list that doesn't show the lookup column and edit the related list web part to use that view.

Use the Edit Form on the List Page

Scenario/Problem: You do not want the user to have to navigate to a separate page or dialog to edit a list item.

Solution: Edit the list page and add the edit form using an InfoPath Form web part.

The InfoPath Form web part can be leveraged to modify the standard list pages to customize the user experience with the list. To accomplish this implementation, follow these steps:

1. Navigate to the list you want to modify.

2. From the Site Actions menu, select Edit Page.

3. Click Add Web Part on the page and select the InfoPath Form Web Part. Click Add.

4. From the list web part on the page, select Connections, Send Row of Data To, InfoPath Form Web Part, as shown in Figure 10.8, to create the connection between the two web parts.

5. In the Choose Connection dialog, select Get Form From, as shown in Figure 10.9. The InfoPath Form web part will receive the edit form from the list web part. Click Finish.

6. Move the InfoPath Form web part below the list web part by dragging it below the list web part, as shown in Figure 10.10.

7. On the Page ribbon bar, click Stop Editing to save the changes.

In browse mode, selecting a list item's double-sided arrow icon displays the InfoPath edit form on the same page, as shown in Figure 10.11. Users may modify the entry right on the list page.

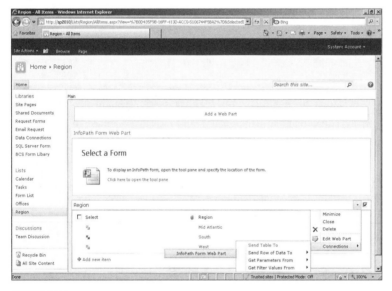

FIGURE 10.8
Sending the row of data to the InfoPath Form web part creates a connection.

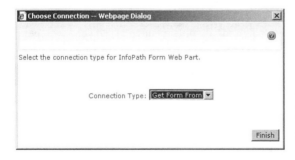

FIGURE 10.9
Selecting Get Form From allows the InfoPath Form web part to receive the form from the list web part.

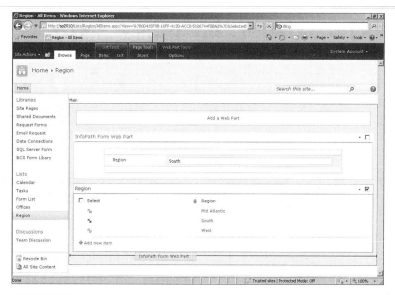

FIGURE 10.10
Dragging the InfoPath Form web part moves it below the list web part.

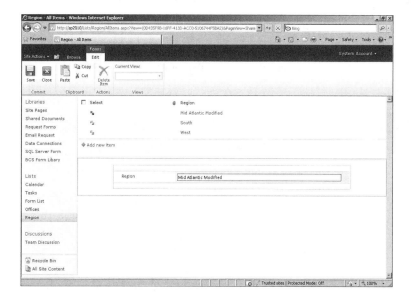

FIGURE 10.11
Selecting a list item displays the Edit Form for that item on the same page.

NOTE   Users who do not have permissions on the list items will not be able to submit any changes. The edit form will still show on the page and appear to be editable, but an error message will appear if the user attempts to save a modification.

Create a Custom List Page That Displays the List Item Form

Scenario/Problem: You need to create a custom list page that displays the list and the list item form.

Solution: Create a new web part page and drag the list and the InfoPath Form web part onto the page. Connect the two web parts.

Modifying the list page in the previous example is neat, but you might not want to do that on the actual list page. Instead, you may want to create a custom list page that performs similar functionality.

To create a custom list page, follow these steps:

1. Create a new view for your list that only displays the main column (for example, Office).

2. Create a new web part page in your SharePoint site using a template that has a left column.

3. Click Add Web Part in the left column zone and select the list from the Library and Lists category, as shown in Figure 10.12, to add the list web part onto the page. Click Add.

4. Click Add Web Part in the right or header column zone and select InfoPath Form Web Part, as shown in Figure 10.13, to add the InfoPath Form web part onto the page. Click Add.

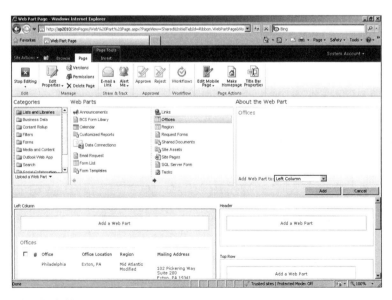

FIGURE 10.12
Selecting the list web part adds the web part to the page.

FIGURE 10.13
Selecting InfoPath Form Web Parts adds the web part to the page.

5. Select Edit Web Part from the list web part item menu. The web part tool pane appears.

6. In the web part tool pane, change the view to the main column view, as shown in Figure 10.14, such that only the main column is displayed in the list web part. Click OK.

FIGURE 10.14
Changing the view determines what is displayed in the list web part.

7. From the list web part on the page, select Connections, Send Row of Data To, InfoPath Form Web Part, as shown in Figure 10.15, to create the connection between the two web parts.

8. In the Choose Connection dialog, select Get Form From, as shown in Figure 10.16. The InfoPath Form web part will receive the edit form from the list web part. Click Finish.

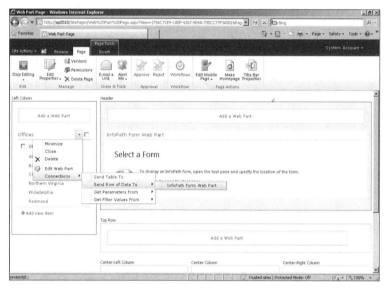

FIGURE 10.15
Sending the row of data to the InfoPath Form web part creates a connection.

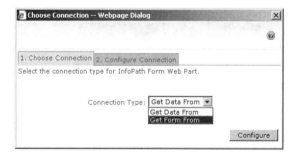

FIGURE 10.16
Selecting Get Form From allows the InfoPath Form web part to receive the form from the list web part.

9. Click Stop Editing on the Page ribbon bar.

10. Selecting an item from the list displays the list edit form in the InfoPath Form web part on the page, as shown in Figure 10.17.

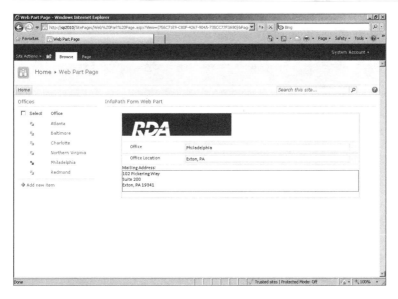

FIGURE 10.17
Selecting a list item displays the details on the page.

> **TIP** Change the Chrome to None on the InfoPath Form web part to hide the web part title or change the title to something more meaningful (for example, Office Details).

Expose Form Fields as Web Part Connection Parameters

> **Scenario/Problem:** You need fields from your form available for web part connectivity when using the form in an InfoPath Form web part.

Solution: Promote the fields in your form as SharePoint web part connection parameters.

There are many opportunities to promote fields as parameters during publishing of the form or creating a "send data to web part" rule action. However, at any time, you may promote fields as web parameters using the form options:

1. From File, Info, click the Form Options button, as shown in Figure 10.18, to access the form settings.

2. Select the Property Promotion category in the Form Options dialog.

3. Click Add in the bottom section and select a field from your form, as shown in Figure 10.19, to use the field as a web part parameter. Select the parameter type and click OK to create the web part parameter.

4. All the fields listed in the box will be available for web part usage, as shown in Figure 10.20. Click OK to save the changes.

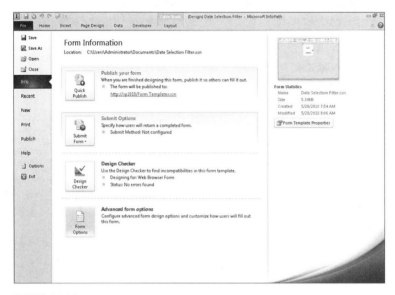

FIGURE 10.18
Clicking Form Options allows you to access the form settings.

FIGURE 10.19
Selecting a field allows you to create the web part parameter.

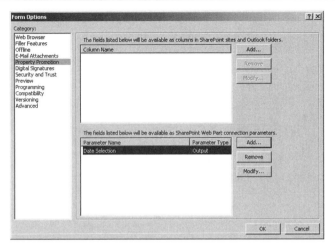

FIGURE 10.20
Clicking OK allows all fields listed to be used as web part parameters.

Create a Form to Send Data to Web Parts

Scenario/Problem: You want to provide the user with an input interface that will send the entered values to other web parts on your page.

Solution: Create a form with inputs and a button that sends data to the web part.

With the InfoPath Form web part, you may create forms that are used solely for input purposes and submit the entered data as parameters to other web parts on the page. A simple example of this is using a form to filter items displayed in a list.

First let's create the form:

1. Create a new form with a date picker control and a button. Name the date field DateSelection and change the button label to Apply. Because this is for a web part, resize the form as shown in Figure 10.21.

2. From File, Info, click the Form Options button.

3. Select the Property Promotion category in the Form Options dialog.

4. Click Add in the bottom section and select the Date field from your form. Select Output as the parameter type and click OK to create the web part parameter.

5. Click OK in the Form Options dialog.

6. Select the Apply button and on the ribbon bar select Add Rule, When This Button Is Clicked, Submit Data, as shown in Figure 10.22, to create a new button rule. The Rule Details dialog appears.

7. In the Rule Details dialog, change the Action to Send Data to Web Part, as shown in Figure 10.23, such that the rule sends the parameters to a connected web part.

8. Optionally, click the Property Promotion button to ensure the Date Selection field is being promoted as a SharePoint web part parameter.

9. Click OK.

10. Publish the form to a SharePoint library or as a content type. If using a content type, add it to an existing form library.

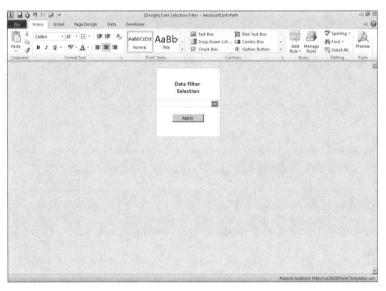

FIGURE 10.21
Resizing the form prepares it for web part usage.

Now let's create the page:

1. Create a new web part page in your SharePoint site. Use a template that has a left column.

2. Add an InfoPath Form web part to the Left Column zone and configure it to use the form you created in the previous steps.

3. Add a List View web part to the Body zone of the page by selecting a form library.

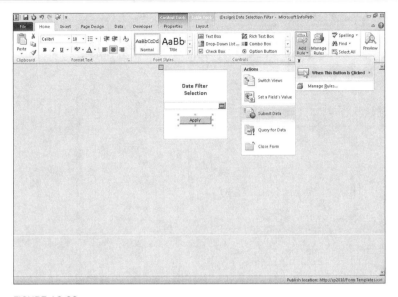

FIGURE 10.22
Clicking Add Rule creates a new button rule.

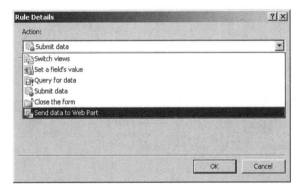

FIGURE 10.23
Changing the action allows the button to send data to a connected web part.

4. From the InfoPath Form Web Part item menu, select Connections, Send Data To, List Name, as shown in Figure 10.24, to create a web part connection between the web parts. The Choose Connection dialog appears.

5. We are using the connection as a filter, so in the Choose Connection dialog, click the Configure button.

6. Select the Date column from the list web part in the Consumer Field Name, as shown in Figure 10.25, to send the Date Selection as a filter to that field.

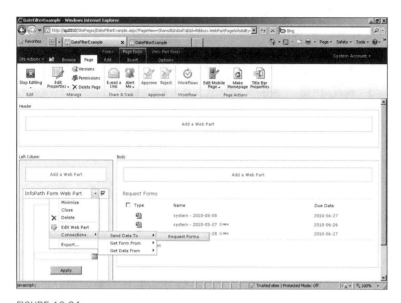

FIGURE 10.24
Sending data to the list web part creates a web part connection.

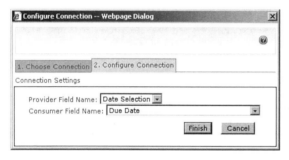

FIGURE 10.25
Selecting the consumer field determines the column that is to be filtered.

7. Click Finish.

8. On the Page ribbon bar, click the Stop Editing button.

9. Enter a date into the form and click Apply. The list shows only (filters) the items with a due date of the entered date, as shown in Figure 10.26.

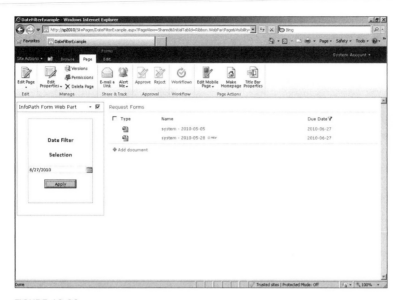

FIGURE 10.26
Entering a date and clicking Apply filters the list.

CHAPTER 11

Using Forms in SharePoint Workflows

This chapter explores workflow scenarios with InfoPath and SharePoint using SharePoint Designer 2010 workflows. InfoPath may also be used in Visual Studio 2010 workflows, which are discussed in Chapter 16, "Leveraging Visual Studio 2010 with InfoPath," within the more technical part of this book.

One of the powerful uses of InfoPath with SharePoint 2010 is the ability to create forms that are used in SharePoint workflows. Workflows help facilitate business processes. They are mostly centered on the processing of information. InfoPath provides the vehicle for retrieving that information and making it useful within the workflow steps.

Create a SharePoint Workflow for a Form Library

> **Scenario/Problem:** You need to create a workflow based on the submission of your form to a form library.

Solution: Use SharePoint Designer 2010 to create a new list workflow.

SharePoint Designer 2010 enables you to easily create workflows against your form library. This is accomplished by creating a new list workflow. To do this, follow these steps:

1. Launch SharePoint Designer 2010 and open your SharePoint site.

2. Select Workflows from the Site Objects list within the left navigation pane.

3. On the ribbon bar, click the List Workflows and select the form library that contains your form, as shown in Figure 11.1, to create the workflow against that library.

> **NOTE** This scenario provides a simple example to get started. The subsequent scenarios enhance the workflow.

4. In the Create List Workflow dialog, enter a name and description to save the workflow, as shown in Figure 11.2. Step 1 appears in the main area.

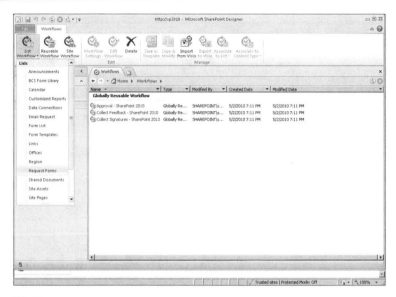

FIGURE 11.1
Selecting the form library creates a workflow using that library.

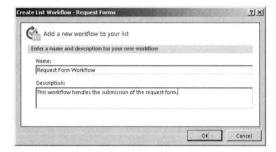

FIGURE 11.2
Entering a workflow name saves the workflow using that name.

5. Click the Action button and select Send an Email, as shown in Figure 11.3, to create an email action.

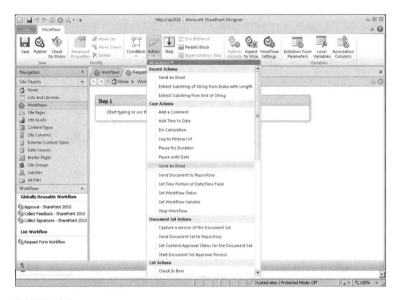

FIGURE 11.3
Selecting Send an Email creates an email action.

6. Click the These Users link to open the email dialog shown in Figure 11.4.

7. Click the address book button next to the To: entry and add the user who created the current item, as shown in Figure 11.5, to address the email to the user who submitted the form. Click OK.

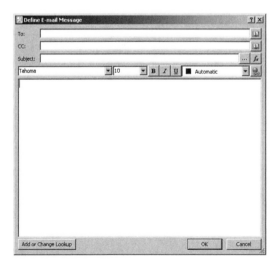

FIGURE 11.4
Clicking the These Users links opens the email dialog.

8. Enter the email subject in the Subject line and fill out the body to complete the email entry, as shown in Figure 11.6. Click OK.

9. Click the workflow breadcrumb in the top the main area next to Editor to display the workflow settings.

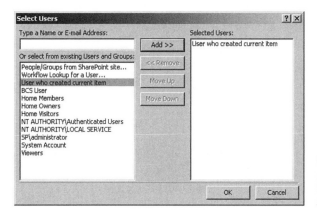

FIGURE 11.5
Adding the user who created the item sends the email to the form submitter.

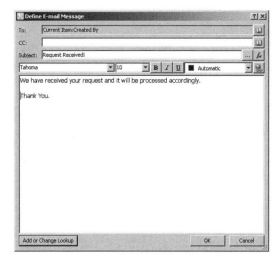

FIGURE 11.6
Entering a subject and filling in the body completes the email entry.

10. Under Start Options, select the Start Workflow Automatically When an Item Is Created option, as shown in Figure 11.7, such that the workflow is kicked off when a user submits a new form.

11. Click the Publish button on the ribbon bar to save and publish the workflow to the form library, as shown in Figure 11.8.

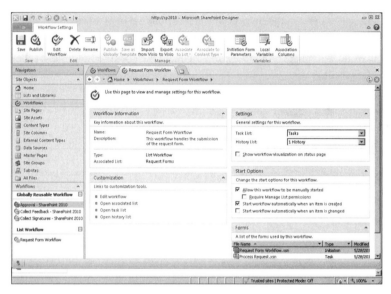

FIGURE 11.7
Selecting the start options initiates the workflow upon form creation.

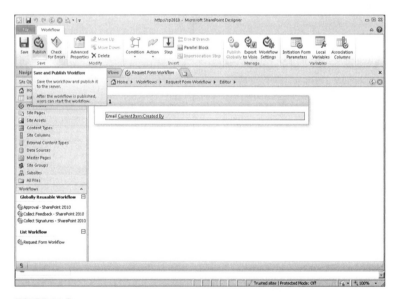

FIGURE 11.8
Clicking Publish saves and publishes the workflow to the form library.

After you have published the workflow, navigate the form library and add a new document. You should receive an email with the subject and body that you configured. As noted in this scenario, the example here is a simple one to get you started with workflows.

Include a Link to the Form in an Email

Scenario/Problem: You want to include a link to the form in an email from a workflow.

Solution: In the body of the email message, add a lookup.

When sending an email to the originator of the form (such as in the previous scenario) or to a person who needs to handle the submitted form, it is always nice to include a link to the form such that the user can easily navigate to the form instance and see the details.

To do this, follow these steps:

1. In the email message dialog from the workflow action, click the Add or Change Lookup button.

2. Ensure that the Data Source is the Current Item. Switch the Field from source entry to Encoded Absolute URL to add the full path of the form into the email message, as shown in Figure 11.9. Click OK.

The lookup function is entered into your email message, as shown in Figure 11.10, and dynamically renders the link for the current item when sending the email.

FIGURE 11.9
Selecting Encoded Absolute URL inserts the full path of the form into the email message.

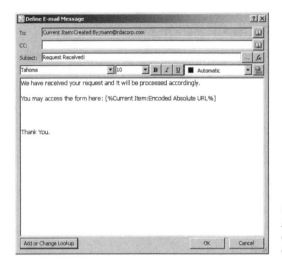

FIGURE 11.10
Adding the lookup function dynamically renders the value from the current item.

Add a Task to the Workflow

A main component of workflow processes is taking action on the submitted form. This is easily facilitated by creating tasks and assigning them to users. To do this, follow these steps:

1. Click in the step in the workflow where you want to create a task item.

> **TIP** If you select the entire step, the Conditions and Actions buttons are disabled. You need to click into the step to add new conditions or actions.

2. Click the Action button on the ribbon bar and select Assign a To-Do Item, as shown in Figure 11.11, to create the task item. The action is added to your step with links.

3. Click the A To-Do Item link. The Custom Task Wizard dialog appears. Click Next.

4. Enter a name for the new task title, as shown in Figure 11.12, and click Finish to create the new task type.

> **TIP** This process is actually creating a new site content type and adds it to the tasks list of your SharePoint site.

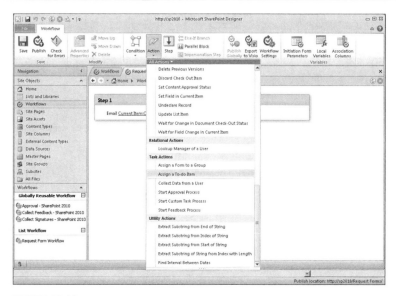

FIGURE 11.11
Selecting Assign a To-Do Item generates a task item.

FIGURE 11.12
Entering a name for the title creates a new type of task.

5. Click the These Users link and select the user or users to assign the task. Click OK.

The completed task action should look similar to Figure 11.13. Publish the workflow and navigate to the form library. Fill out and submit a new form to test the workflow. A new task is created in the Tasks list, as shown in Figure 11.14. Complete the task to complete the workflow.

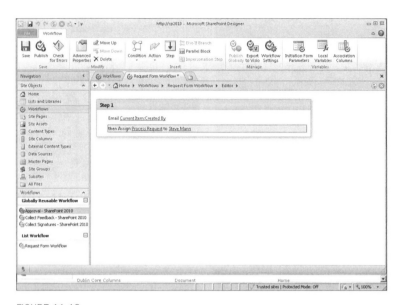

FIGURE 11.13
Configuring the task and the users completes the task action.

TIP The workflow will not continue or complete until the task is completed.

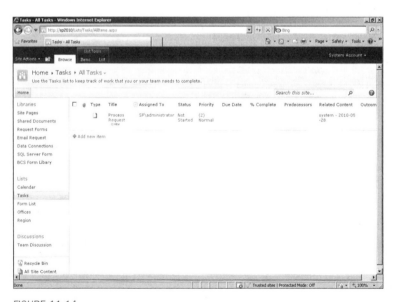

FIGURE 11.14
Initiating the workflow creates a new task in the Tasks list.

Perform Workflow Actions Based on Form Values

Scenario/Problem: You need to perform actions in your workflow based on entered values of the form.

Solution: Add a condition to the workflow step.

Many times you need to perform actions only if values entered on the form meet certain conditions. This can easily be implemented using conditions in your workflow.

To perform an action based on a condition, follow these steps:

1. Click in the step in the workflow where you want to perform the conditional action.

2. Click the Condition button on the ribbon bar and select If Current Item Field Equals Value, as shown in Figure 11.15, to create the condition. The condition is added to your step with links.

3. Click the field link and select a field from the form, as shown in Figure 11.16, to base the condition on that field's value. For this example, the Amount field is used.

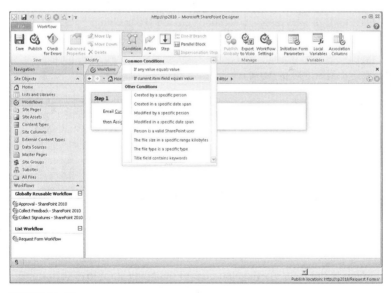

FIGURE 11.15
Selecting a condition item adds the condition to the workflow step.

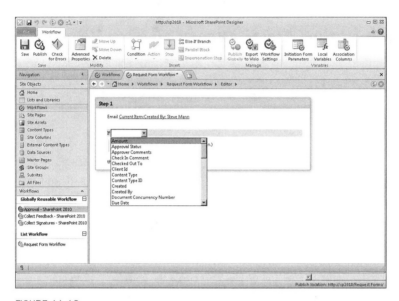

FIGURE 11.16
Selecting a field bases the condition on that field's value.

4. When using a numeric value field such as the Amount field in this example, you may change the comparison details by clicking the Equals link, as shown in Figure 11.17. For this example, select the Is Greater Than comparison.

5. Click the Value link to enter the value to compare to the field value, as shown in Figure 11.18. For this example, we'll check to see whether the amount is greater than $500 and enter 500 in the text box.

> **TIP** Notice the Function button next to the text box. Instead of hard coding a value, you may enter a formula or other workflow value to produce a dynamic comparison.

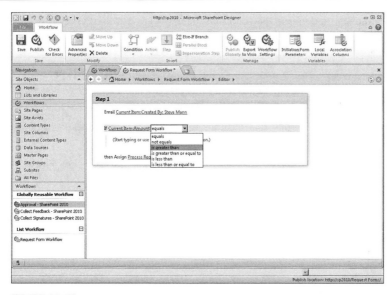

FIGURE 11.17
Clicking the Equals link allows you to change the comparison.

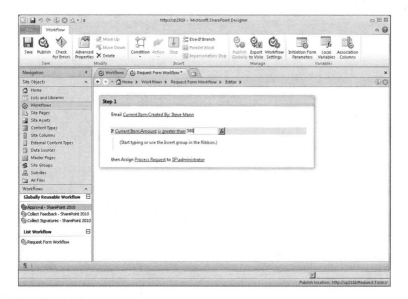

FIGURE 11.18
Clicking the Value link allows you to enter a value to compare to the field value.

6. Click in the row underneath the condition statement and enter To in the text box. Click the magnifying glass button or press the Enter key. A list of available actions appear in a drop-down, as shown in Figure 11.19.

7. Select the Assign a To-Do Item option. For this example, we'll need approval for requests that have an amount over $500 before we continue with the normal workflow processes.

8. Click the A To-Do Item link. The Custom Task Wizard dialog appears. Click Next.

9. Enter a name for the new task title, such as Approve Request, and click Finish to create the new task type.

10. Click the These Users link and select the user or users to assign the task. Click OK. The workflow step should now look similar to Figure 11.20 and contain the completed condition such that amounts over 500 need to be approved first via an approval task.

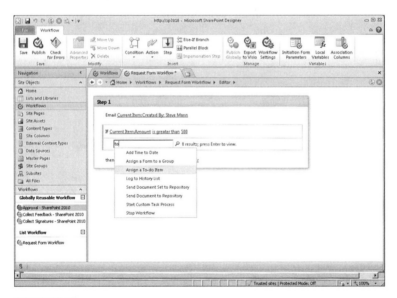

FIGURE 11.19
Entering text produces a list of available actions.

11. Publish the workflow.

12. Navigate to the form library and submit a new document with a value that meets the condition. The Approve Request task is created in the Tasks list and must be completed first, as shown in Figure 11.21.

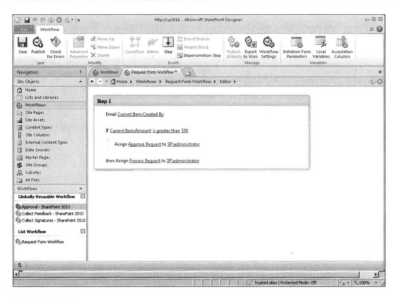

FIGURE 11.20
Completing the condition produces an approval task.

FIGURE 11.21
Submitting a form with a value that meets the condition generates the approve task.

Perform One Workflow Action or Another (But Not Both)

Scenario/Problem: You need to perform either one action or another depending on a certain condition.

Solution: Add an else-if branch to the step.

You may use the else-if branch to string together logic in your condition. The first application of this functionality produces an Else section to your condition. This allows you to perform one action if a condition is met or otherwise perform another action.

To apply the else-if branch to a condition, follow these steps:

1. Select an If condition in your step.

2. Click the Else-If Branch button on the ribbon bar, as shown in Figure 11.22, to create add the Else section.

3. Add actions to the Else section as needed.

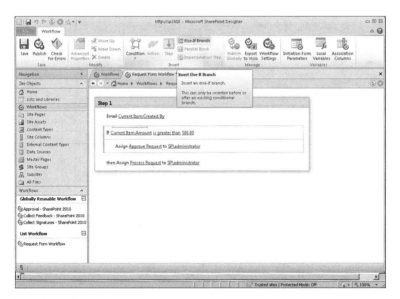

FIGURE 11.22
Clicking the Else-If Branch button adds an Else section to your condition.

If you have an action defined already that needs to be in your Else section, simply select Move Action Up from the item menu, as shown in Figure 11.23. You now have a complete if-else block of logic in the workflow step, as shown in Figure 11.24.

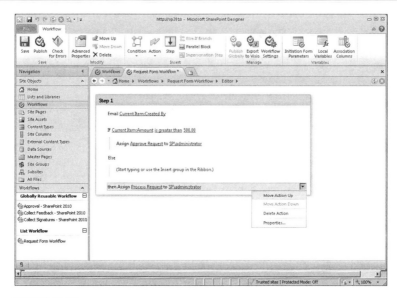

FIGURE 11.23
Selecting Move Action Up moves the action into the Else section.

FIGURE 11.24
Using the else-if branch with actions completes an if-else block.

TIP Add another condition rather than an action in the Else section to produce the actual else-if branch.

Get a User from a People/Group Picker Control

Scenario/Problem: You would like to use the user accounts that were entered into a people/group picker control.

Solution: Promote the AccountID field when publishing your form. Use Merge to combine multiple entries.

When publishing your form, you need to expose the account field that is used in the people/group picker control. You may expose the field at any time using the Property Promotion option in Form Options.

To do this, follow these steps:

1. From File, Info, click the Form Options button, as shown in Figure 11.25, to access the form settings.

2. Select the Property Promotion category in the Form Options dialog.

3. Click Add in the top section and select the AccountID from the Person group of your form, as shown in Figure 11.26, to expose the field to the list and workflow.

4. If your people/group picker control allows multiple selections, select the Merge option. If your people/group picker control doesn't allow multiple selections, select the First option.

5. Click OK on the Select a Field or Group dialog.

6. Click OK on the Form Options dialog.

7. Publish your form.

FIGURE 11.25
Clicking Form Options allows you to access the form settings.

FIGURE 11.26
Selecting a field allows you to expose it
to your list and workflow.

> **TIP** If your workflow is open in SharePoint Designer while making changes to the
> form or list, right-click the workflow tab and select Refresh such that the workflow
> recognizes any changes.

In the workflow, you may now select users from the exposed field. Typically, this is
accomplished by selecting Workflow Lookup for a User in the Select Users dialog,
as shown Figure 11.27, and clicking Add. Selecting the exposed field from the
current item will use the accounts entered in the people/group picker, as shown in
Figure 11.28.

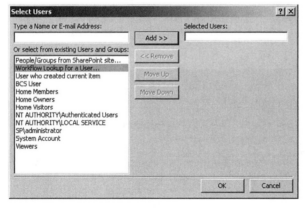

FIGURE 11.27
Selecting Workflow Lookup
for a User allows you to
select a field that contains a
user account.

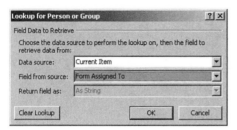

FIGURE 11.28

Selecting the exposed field from the current item will use the accounts entered.

Customize the Task Form

Scenario/Problem: You would like to customize the system generated task form used in your workflow.

Solution: From the workflow properties screen, click the Task form in the Forms section. Modify the form, save it, and publish it back to SharePoint.

The workflow properties page displays the forms that are used in your workflow, as shown in Figure 11.29.

TIP The workflow properties page appears when opening your workflow. To get to it while editing the workflow, simply select your workflow name in the breadcrumb-style menu underneath the Workflow tab.

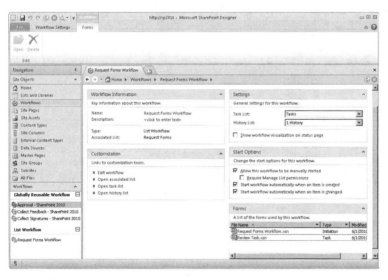

FIGURE 11.29

The forms that are used in your workflow are displayed in the workflow properties page.

Clicking the task form opens it within InfoPath Designer. Modify the form as needed and save a local copy. Use the Quick Publish option to publish the form back to SharePoint.

Add Form Parameters Used When Starting Your Workflow

> **Scenario/Problem:** You need to capture information when your workflow is started manually.

Solution: Add initiation form parameters using the Initiation Form Parameters button.

Initiation form parameters are fields that are collected upon the manual starting of your workflow. Adding initiation form parameters adds those fields to the system generated imitation form.

To add initiation form parameters to your workflow, follow these steps:

1. From the workflow editor, click the Initiation Form Parameters button on the Workflow ribbon bar, as shown in Figure 11.30. The Association and Initiation Form Parameters dialog appears.

2. Click Add. The Add Field dialog appears.

3. Enter a field name and select the information as shown in Figure 11.31 to configure the new field. Click Next.

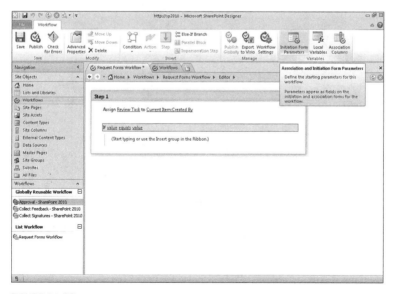

FIGURE 11.30
Clicking the Initiation Form Parameters button allows you to add initiation fields.

4. Enter a default value for the field in the Column Settings dialog and click Finish.

5. Click OK on the Association and Initiation Form Parameters dialog.

6. Publish the workflow to save the changes.

FIGURE 11.31

Entering a name and information type configures the new field.

7. Click the initiation form in the forms section of the workflow properties page to view the form changes in InfoPath, as shown in Figure 11.32. The new field is added to the initiation form.

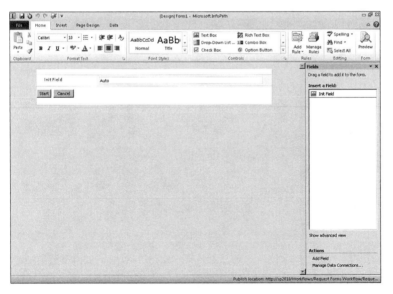

FIGURE 11.32

Adding a new initiation field adds it to the workflow initiation form.

You may now use the field within your workflow by selecting it from the Workflow Variables and Parameters data source, as shown in Figure 11.33, when performing a workflow lookup.

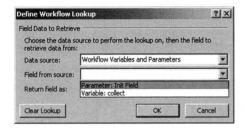

FIGURE 11.33

Selecting the Workflow Variables and Parameters data source allows you to select the initiation form field.

CHAPTER 12

Enhancing the User Experience

This chapter demonstrates ways to improve the user experience with your forms by leveraging InfoPath controls, functionality, and settings. Designing intuitive and easy-to-use forms facilitates their acceptance within an organization.

Display a Read-Only Value

Scenario/Problem: You have a read-only value to display on your form.

Solution: Display the value in a text box that is set to read-only and does not contain any borders or shading.

When a read-only field is displayed in a text box, you obviously do not want the user to edit that field. You also do not want the user to think that they can edit that field. Therefore, it's best to modify the text box properties accordingly.

To display a read-only value, follow these steps:

1. Right-click the text box that contains the read-only field on your form and select Text Box Properties, as shown in Figure 12.1, to display the properties dialog.

2. Click the Display tab and check the Read-Only box, as shown in Figure 12.2, to make the text box read-only. Click OK.

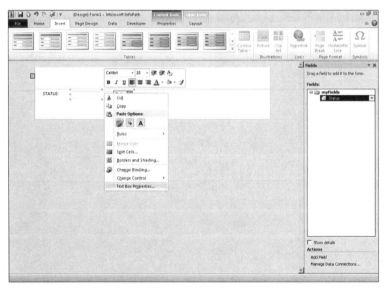

FIGURE 12.1
Selecting Text Box Properties displays the Properties dialog.

FIGURE 12.2

Checking the Read-Only box makes the text box read-only.

3. Right-click the text box again and select Borders and Shading, as shown in Figure 12.3, to modify the borders and shading properties.

4. On the Borders tab, click the None button to remove the borders from the text box, as shown in Figure 12.4.

5. Click the Shading tab and select No Color to remove any shading from the text box, as shown in Figure 12.5. Click OK.

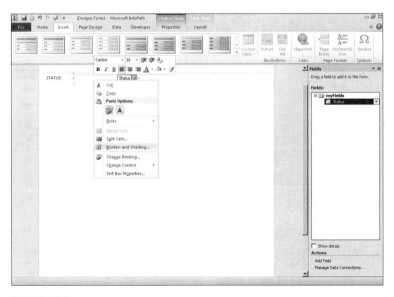

FIGURE 12.3

Selecting Borders and Shading allows you to modify the borders and shading properties.

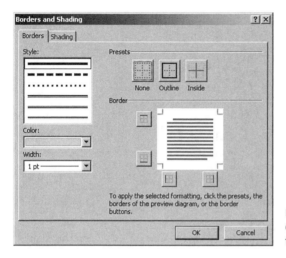

FIGURE 12.4
Clicking the None button removes the borders from the text box.

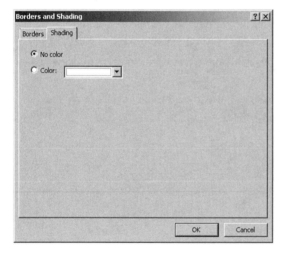

FIGURE 12.5
Select No Color removes the shading from the text box.

Previewing or rendering your form displays the field as read-only, as shown in Figure 12.6.

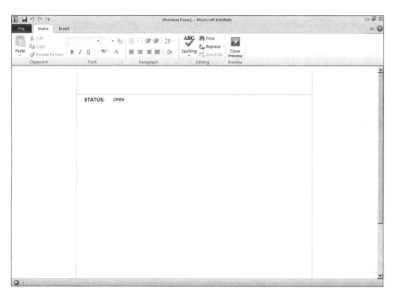

FIGURE 12.6
Rendering the form displays the field as read-only.

Compact Sections of Fields/Controls

Scenario/Problem: You have many related fields to present to the user and want to reduce the length of your form.

Solution: Use a four-column table layout to compact the sections of similar fields.

When you have sections of similar fields on your form, it is a recommended best practice to use one of the four-column table layouts. To use a four-column table layout in your form or section, select the Tables menu on the Insert ribbon bar and select one of the four-column layouts, as shown in Figure 12.7.

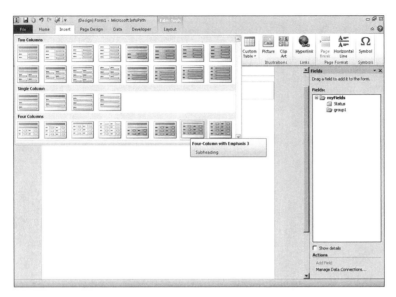

FIGURE 12.7
Selecting a table layout inserts the table into your form or section.

Configure Dynamic Sections

Scenario/Problem: You have optional information that must be filled out only if another option is selected.

Solution: Create a rule to show only the optional sections when another field value is selected.

Hiding or showing sections is another recommended method to enhance the user experience. Optional or conditional fields should only be shown if needed. Although this can be implemented by using optional section controls, it is more aesthetic to use a check box to control the visibility of the optional section.

To do this, follow these steps:

1. On your form, add a check box control and a section control, as shown in Figure 12.8. (Optionally, you may add fields within the section, but that is not necessary to wire up the rule.) The check box will control the visibility of the section.

2. Select the section on your form and click Manage Rules on the Home ribbon bar. The Rules pane appears.

3. In the Rules pane, click New and select Formatting, as shown in Figure 12.9, to add a new visibility rule.

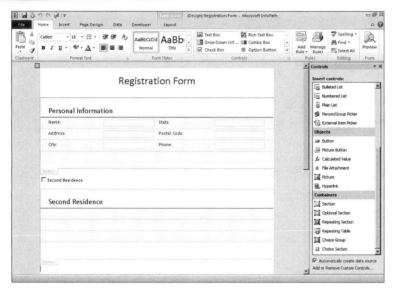

FIGURE 12.8
Adding a check box and a section to your form allows you to control the dynamic section.

4. Enter a rule name and click None in the Condition section. The Condition dialog appears.

5. In the Condition dialog, enter the condition such that the value of the check box is not equal to True, as shown in Figure 12.10, to determine when the section control will be hidden. Click OK.

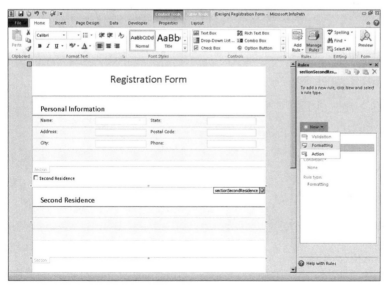

FIGURE 12.9
Selecting Formatting allows you to create a visibility rule.

FIGURE 12.10
Setting the condition determines when the section control will be hidden.

6. In the Rules pane, click the Hide This Control check box to set the formatting action of the rule, as shown in Figure 12.11.

7. Preview your form to test the rule. Initially, the section is not visible, but if you check the check box, the conditional section appears, as shown in Figure 12.12.

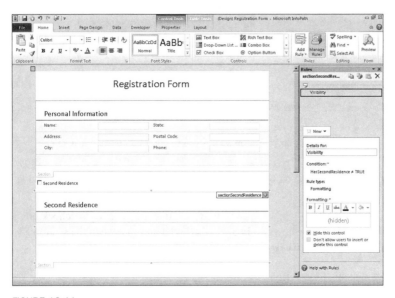

FIGURE 12.11
Checking Hide This Control configures the formatting action of the rule.

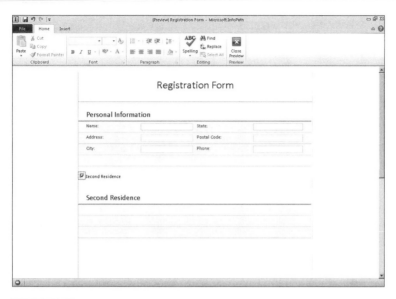

FIGURE 12.12
Checking the check box displays the conditional section.

Make Screen Tips Informative for Validation

Scenario/Problem: You have fields on your form that have validation rules that require screen tip text.

Solution: Include the format that the field needs to conform to in the screen tip.

When using validation rules (see Chapter 4, "SharePoint Form Rules," for creating rules), the entered values must conform to the configured pattern. If users do not know the format expected, they can become frustrated, and you don't want to leave them guessing.

Therefore, it is a recommended best practice to include the required format (of the value) within the screen tip to provide the user with the expected entry pattern, as shown in Figure 12.13.

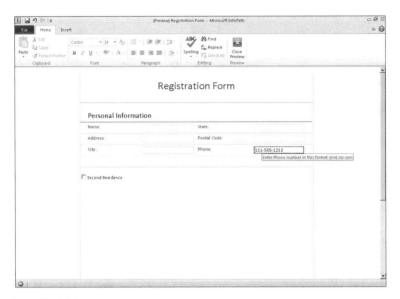

FIGURE 12.13
Including the required format of the value provides the user with expected entry pattern.

Notify the User of Successful Submission

Scenario/Problem: You want to notify the user that the form has been submitted successfully.

Solution: Use a confirmation view to notify the user of a successful submission.

After submitting a form, the user may or may not know that the information has been successfully received by SharePoint. Therefore, it is a best practice to create a confirmation view that is displayed after form submission.

The first steps required to create and configure a confirmation view is to set up the submit options:

1. On the Data ribbon bar, click Submit Options. The Submit Options dialog appears.

2. In the Submit Options dialog, select the Perform Custom Actions Using Rules option, as shown in Figure 12.14, to configure the submission of the form.

3. For this example, click the Advanced button and change the After Submit to Leave the Form Open, as shown in Figure 12.15, to configure what occurs after submission.

4. Click OK.

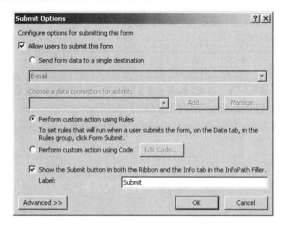

FIGURE 12.14
Submit options allow you to configure the submission of the form.

That takes care of the submit options, but now you need to configure the form submit rule. For this example, you will need to create a new view (see Chapter 6, "SharePoint Form Page Design and Views") named Confirmation View, which should contain a submit confirmation message and a button that closes the form.

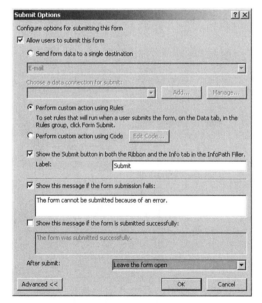

FIGURE 12.15
The After Submit option configures what occurs after submission.

To enter the submit rule, follow these steps:

1. On the Data ribbon bar, click Form Submit in the Rules section. The Rules pane appears.

2. Click New and select Action.

3. Enter Submit Form as the name of the rule.

4. Click Add and select Submit Data. The Rule Details dialog appears, as shown in Figure 12.16, which allows you to configure the connection.

5. Select the data connection to submit the form. (If you don't have a data connection configured, see Chapter 2, "Creating a SharePoint Form with InfoPath Designer," for an example.) Click OK. Your submit rule should look similar to Figure 12.17, which ensures the form will be submitted.

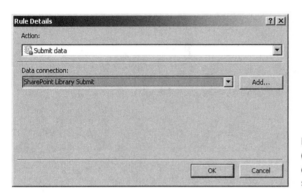

FIGURE 12.16
Configuring the connection determines where it will be submitted.

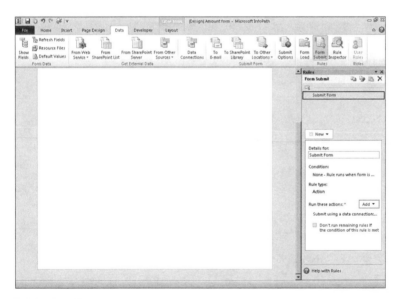

FIGURE 12.17
Configuring one rule to submit the form ensures it will be submitted.

6. Click Add again to add another action. Select Switch Views. In the Rules Details dialog, change the view to the Confirmation View, as shown in Figure 12.18, to determine which view to be displayed. Click OK. Your form submit rule should now look similar to Figure 12.19, which implements two actions upon form submission.

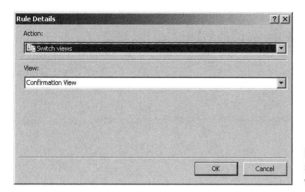

FIGURE 12.18
Selecting a view determines
which one will be displayed.

FIGURE 12.19
The form submit rule implements two actions upon form submission.

7. Save and Publish your form to SharePoint. Once your form is published to SharePoint, you may create a new instance and test the rules. Submitting the form displays the confirmation view, as shown in Figure 12.20.

FIGURE 12.20
Submitting the form displays the confirmation view.

Create a Tabbed Navigation in Your Form

Scenario/Problem: You want to provide a tabbed navigation for your form.

Solution: Use picture buttons and views to display different sets of fields in your form.

When there are many different groups of unrelated entries in your form, it is recommended to create separate views to handle the display and entry of each group of fields. An aesthetically pleasing way to handle the switching between the views is through a tabbed navigation.

The initial setup of the tabbed navigation requires the following:

1. Create a view in your form for each tab you will have.

2. Create two image files for each tab, one for when the tab is selected and one when it is not selected. The selected version will also be used for the hover picture.

TIP Use PowerPoint 2010 to create the pictures for your picture buttons. Right-clicking a PowerPoint object allows you to save it as an external picture file!

3. Drag a picture button for each tab you will have onto your first view.

4. Configure the first button to use the selected version of the first tab image.

5. Configure the other buttons to use the nonselected version of the images as the picture and the selected versions of the images as the hover picture. The initial setup should look similar to Figure 12.21

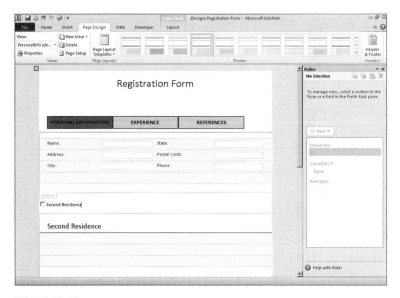

FIGURE 12.21
Adding and configuring the picture buttons provides the basis for the tabbed navigation.

6. Copy and paste the picture buttons from the main view onto the other views.

7. Reconfigure the buttons on each view such that the current view tab has the selected picture with no hover picture. The first button needs to be configured back to the unselected image as the main picture and the selected image as the hover picture, as shown in Figure 12.22, to provide the selection experience.

TIP Set all margins on the picture buttons to zero (0) so that they can be placed together without any gaps of whitespace between them.

Now that the buttons and views have been configured, we now need to hook up the rules to provide the navigation actions to the tab. You can add the necessary fields to the other views, but that is not required to implement the tabbed navigation.

To implement the navigation, follow these steps:

1. On the first view, select the second button.

2. Click Manage Rules on the Home ribbon bar.

3. In the Rules pane, click New, Action to create a new action rule.

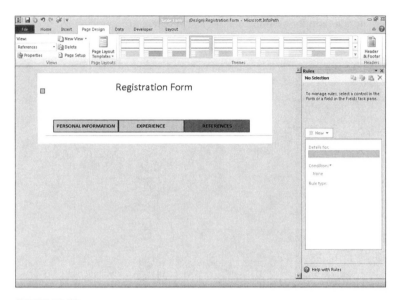

FIGURE 12.22
Configuring the picture buttons on each view provides the selection experience.

4. In the Run These Actions section, click Add and select Switch Views to create a switch view action, as shown in Figure 12.23.

5. In the Rule Details dialog, select the view that corresponds to the button, as shown in Figure 12.24, such that when the button is clicked, the appropriate view is displayed. Click OK.

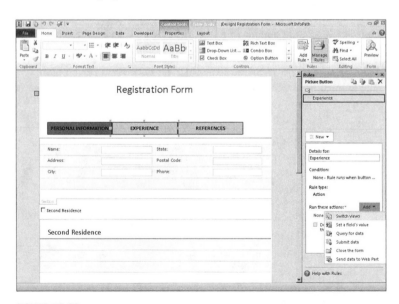

FIGURE 12.23
Selecting Switch Views creates a switch view action.

6. Use the copy/paste buttons in the Rules pane (Figure 12.25) to copy the rule you just created.

7. Select the next picture button and click the paste button in the Rules pane to paste a copy of the rule.

FIGURE 12.24
Selecting the view determines which view is displayed when the button is clicked.

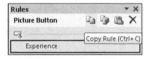

FIGURE 12.25
Using the copy/paste buttons allows you to easily copy rules to other controls.

8. Correct the name of the rule and click the Switch to View action link to change the view to the current button view.

9. Switch to the other views of the form and paste the rule on the nonselected buttons. Change the rule names and actions accordingly.

That's it! Preview your form and click the buttons. The corresponding views display based on the button you click.

TIP Use the button properties to make each button the same height and width. This provides a smoother transition between views.

Use Pictures as Choices

Scenario/Problem: You want to provide pictures as a choice mechanism on your form.

Solution: Use picture buttons within multiple sections to set the values and show the appropriate selections.

Using picture buttons as options is a great way to jazz up your form and provide a great user experience. This can be implemented using a picture button for each option within small sections that are configured to display based on the selected option.

To set this up, follow these steps:

1. First, add the field that will be the option and store the selected value. For example purposes, I am adding a PhoneType field with a default value of Home, as shown in Figure 12.26.

2. The next step is to create image files for each option along with a selected version of the image (similar to the tabbed navigation scenario). For this example, I will use a home and a cell phone image.

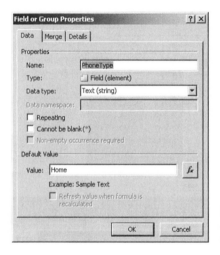

FIGURE 12.26
Adding a field allows you to store the selected value.

3. For each option, create a new section in your form to house the picture buttons as shown in Figure 12.27. In my example, I created a sectionHomePhone and a sectionCellPhone.

4. Create picture buttons inside each section using the selected version of the image for the corresponding section as shown in Figure 12.28. This provides the selected appearance. In my example, the selected home image is in the section-HomePhone section and the selected cell phone image is in the sectionCellPhone section.

TIP   You can use the Hover Picture settings here, too!

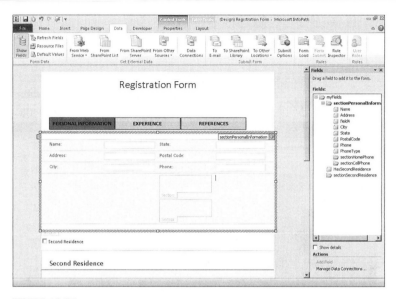

FIGURE 12.27
Creating new sections for each option provides the housing of the picture buttons.

FIGURE 12.28
Placing the selected images within the corresponding section provides the selected appearance.

Now you need to set the actions of the picture buttons by adding the appropriate rules:

1. In the first section, select a non-elected picture button. For my example, I selected the cell phone image.

2. Add a rule to the button with the Set a Field's Value action and set the field for your choice to the appropriate value, as shown in Figure 12.29. This is the value that will be set when the picture button is clicked. For my example, I am setting the PhoneType to Cell.

3. Repeat steps 1-2 for any other nonselected picture buttons in the first section.

4. Repeat steps 1-3 for each additional section. In my sectionCellPhone section, I selected the home button and added the appropriate rule to set the PhoneType to Home.

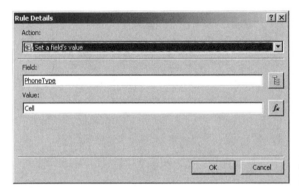

FIGURE 12.29
Setting the field's value changes the value when the button is clicked.

The final set of steps involve creating formatting rules on each section as follows:

1. Select the first section and add a new formatting rule.

2. Add a condition for the rule such that the field is not equal to the value that the section represents, as shown in Figure 12.30, because we are going to hide the section. In my example, for sectionHomePhone, the condition is the PhoneType is not equal to Home.

3. Check the Hide This Control option in the rule under the Formatting section.

4. Repeat steps 1-3 for each additional section.

FIGURE 12.30
Setting the condition hides the section when the field is not equal to the value.

Preview the form the test the implementation. Clicking a nonselected picture changes that button to the selected option, as shown in Figure 12.31.

FIGURE 12.31
Clicking a nonselected picture changes that button to the selected option.

> **TIP** Use a read-only text box to change the label of any dependent fields based on the selected option. In Figure 12.31, notice that the phone label now states Cell Phone.

CHAPTER 13

Leveraging the SharePoint Workspace

This chapter explores the use of the SharePoint Workspace for offline form access. Using the SharePoint Workspace allows a user to access lists and libraries from SharePoint while offline. This also means users may access the SharePoint forms associated to those lists and libraries.

Form libraries cannot be synchronized, and therefore any forms associated with those libraries are available only online.

Synchronize Your List or Site

Scenario/Problem: You need to work with the lists in your site offline.

Solution: Synchronize the lists or entire site to the SharePoint Workspace.

You may easily create an offline workspace of your site by selecting Synchronize to SharePoint Workspace from the Site Actions menu of a site, as shown in Figure 13.1

FIGURE 13.1
Selecting Synchronize to SharePoint Workspace creates an offline workspace of your site.

A prompt appears the first time if a workspace has not yet been created, as shown in Figure 13.2. Click OK to create the workspace and synchronize the contents with SharePoint. You may also need to create a new SharePoint Workspace account if this is the first time you have used the service.

FIGURE 13.2
Clicking OK creates the initial workspace and synchronizes the contents with SharePoint.

You may also synchronize at the list level by using the button on the List ribbon bar, as shown in Figure 13.3, to synchronize the current list.

FIGURE 13.3
Selecting Sync to SharePoint Workspace from the List menu synchronizes the current list.

View Your List and Display Form Offline

Scenario/Problem: You need to view the offline version of your list.

Solution: Select the list in SharePoint Workspace.

Open SharePoint Workspace locally and select the list you want to view. The list items are displayed. Selecting a list item displays the contents within the list's display form, as shown in Figure 13.4.

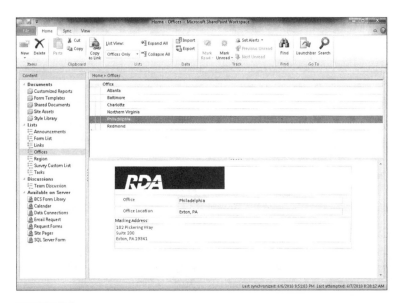

FIGURE 13.4
Selecting a list item displays the contents within the display form.

> **TIP**   If your list forms use any secondary data sources, make sure they are config-
> ured to store a copy of the data in the form for offline access. Otherwise, your list
> forms may not render offline properly.

Edit a List Item Using the Edit Form Offline

Scenario/Problem: You need to edit a list item offline.

Solution: Double-click the list item in SharePoint Workspace.

Double-clicking a list item displays the edit form associated to your list and allows the
user to edit the contents of the list item offline, as shown in Figure 13.5

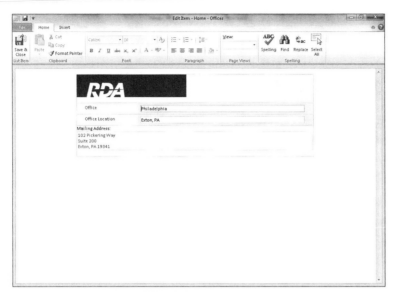

FIGURE 13.5
Double-clicking a list item displays the edit form for editing the contents

Create a New List Item Using the New Form Offline

Scenario/Problem: You need to create a new list item offline.

Solution: On the Home ribbon in SharePoint Workspace, click New.

Clicking New on the Home ribbon opens the new form associated to the list, as shown in Figure 13.6. Enter the values for the new list item and click Save & Close on the top ribbon bar to save a new item offline.

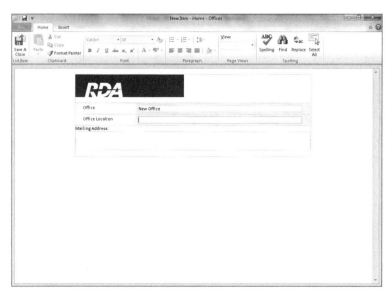

FIGURE 13.6
Clicking New opens the new form associated to your list.

Synchronize Offline Changes to SharePoint

Scenario/Problem: You need to synchronize offline list changes back to the actual SharePoint list.

Solution: Reconnect to the network or use the Sync ribbon bar in SharePoint Workspace.

Once SharePoint Workspace recognizes the SharePoint site, it will automatically synchronize the changes performed offline with the live SharePoint items. You may also force the synchronization manually by using the Sync ribbon bar in SharePoint Workspace.

Synchronizing the list updates any modified items or creates any new items that were entered offline, as shown in Figure 13.7.

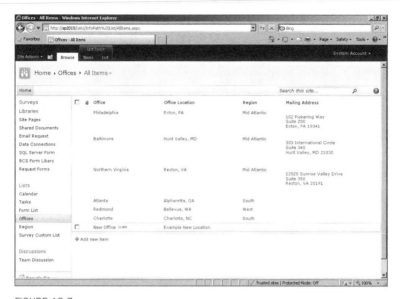

FIGURE 13.7
Synchronizing the list creates the new items entered offline.

CHAPTER 14

Using Template Parts to Create Reusable Form Components

This chapter explains how to create and leverage form template parts. Form template parts provide an easy way to create common controls, fields, and data connections that may be used across multiple forms.

If many forms in your organization require the same data connections and controls, for example, it makes sense to place all the common items into a form template part. Then, you can leverage the template part to reuse the common items without having to create them each time you need a new form.

Your form template parts actually become custom controls that you may use in your forms just like any other controls. All the steps and scenarios are defined here.

Create a New Template Part

> **Scenario/Problem:** You need to create a new template part.

Solution: From File, New, select Blank from the Template Parts section.

The first step in creating a new template part is selecting the Blank template in the Template Parts section from the File, New menu page, as shown in Figure 14.1.

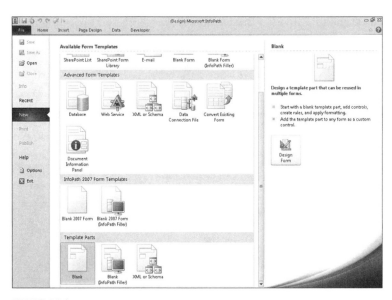

FIGURE 14.1
Selecting the Blank template creates a new template part.

Add Common Data Connections

Scenario/Problem: You need to add data connections to your template part.

Solution: Use the Data ribbon bar menu to add the appropriate data connections.

You may only add data connections to receive data and not to submit data. Adding data connections to your template part is the same process as if you were using data connections in a SharePoint form. It is best to leverage data connection files already created and deployed to your SharePoint site. See Chapter 9, "Using Data in SharePoint Forms," for more information about creating data connections.

TIP If you do not have data connection files available, it is best to create your data connections in the template part and then convert them to connection files.

Add Common Controls

Scenario/Problem: You need to add controls to your template part.

Solution: Use the Control box to add controls to your template part.

Add controls to your template part just as you would a SharePoint form. Use appropriate table layouts accordingly to arrange the controls on your template part.

TIP The size of the template part will be the size of the resultant control on your SharePoint forms. Use space sparingly.

Add Common Fields

Scenario/Problem: You need to add fields to your template part.

Solution: From the Fields pane, add new fields to your template part's Main data structure.

Sometimes you need to have fields that are not bound to controls in your template part. Add any additional fields to your main data source just as you would in normal SharePoint forms.

Save Your Form Template Part

Scenario/Problem: You need to save your form template part.

Solution: Select Save or Save As from the File menu.

Saving your form template part creates a file with a .xtp2 extension. Click File, Save to save your template part. Enter a name and click OK, as shown in Figure 14.2.

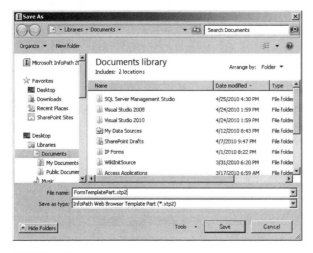

FIGURE 14.2
Saving the form template part creates a .xtp2 file.

TIP After your template part is ready for primetime, you may want to save it to a SharePoint library to share with your team.

Add Your Template Part as a Custom Control

Scenario/Problem: You want to make the form template part available for use.

Solution: Add your form template part as a custom control.

After you have saved your template part, you may add it as one of the InfoPath controls such that each time you design a new form, your template part is available for use.

To add your template part to InfoPath, follow these steps:

1. From InfoPath Designer, expand the Controls menu from the Home top ribbon bar.

2. Select Add or Remove Custom Controls, as shown in Figure 14.3, to open the Add or Remove Custom Controls dialog. The dialog appears as shown in Figure 14.4 and allows you to manage your template parts.

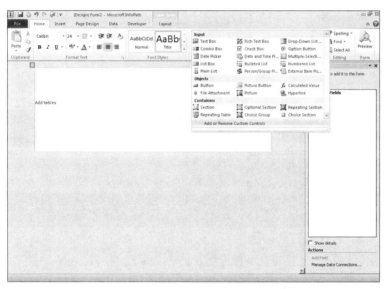

FIGURE 14.3
Selecting Add or Remove Custom Controls opens the custom control dialog.

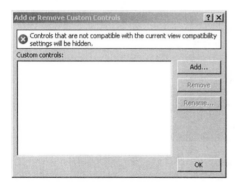

FIGURE 14.4
The custom controls dialog allows you to manage your template parts.

3. Click the Add button. The Add Custom Control Wizard appears, as shown in Figure 14.5, and steps you through the template part addition.

4. Leave the Template Part option selected and click Next.

5. Browse to the xtp2 file you created when saving your template part and click Finish, as shown in Figure 14.6, to add that part as a custom control.

6. Click Close on the confirmation window.

7. Click OK on the Add or Remove Custom Controls dialog.

Your form template part is now available in the Controls list, as shown in Figure 14.7, and may be used in SharePoint forms.

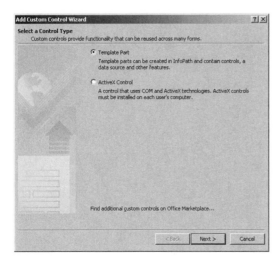

FIGURE 14.5
Clicking Add invokes the Add Custom Control Wizard.

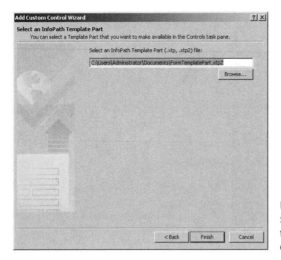

FIGURE 14.6
Selecting the file determines which template part to add as a custom control.

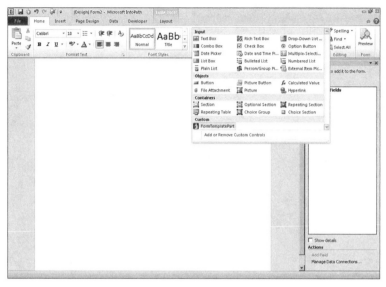

FIGURE 14.7
Adding a template part displays it as an available control to be used in SharePoint forms.

Use Your Template Part as a Control

Scenario/Problem: You want to use your form template part in a SharePoint form.

Solution: Drag your template part control onto your form.

After you have added your template part as a custom control, you may use it like any other control. Dragging the template part onto your form adds the control to your form, as shown in Figure 14.8. The controls and fields from your template part are added to the form, as well.

TIP In your template part, you should rename the myFields main data source to the name of your template part such that when using it in a form, the fields group is more descriptive.

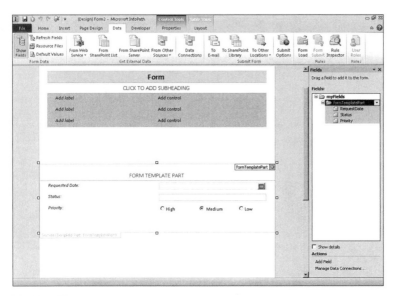

FIGURE 14.8
Dragging your template part onto your form adds the controls and fields.

Change the Name of Your Custom Control

Scenario/Problem: You want to change the name that appears in the Controls list for your form template part.

Solution: In your form template part, modify the template part properties.

The custom control name defaults to the filename of your template part but often times there are no spaces and it may not be the name you want displayed in the control box.

To modify the custom control name used for your template part, follow these steps:

1. With your form template part file opened in InfoPath Designer, select File, Info to display the Form Information screen, as shown in Figure 14.9.

2. Click the Template Part Properties button to display the Template Part Properties dialog.

3. Enter a new name for the form template control, as shown in Figure 14.10, and click OK. This determines what name appears in the controls box.

4. Click File, Save to save the changes to your form template part file.

TIP Use a control name that is descriptive and clear to others if you intend to share your form template part.

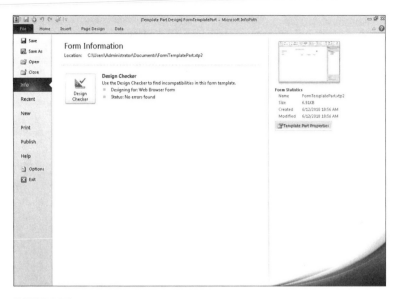

FIGURE 14.9
Select File, Info to display the Form Information screen.

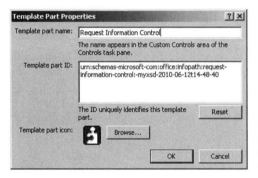

FIGURE 14.10
Entering a name for the template part determines the control name in the controls box.

NOTE You will need to remove the old template part custom control and add the new one to see the name changes.

Change the Icon of Your Custom Control

Scenario/Problem: You want to change the icon that appears in the Controls list for your form template part.

Solution: In your form template part, modify the template part properties.

The custom control icon defaults to the InfoPath template part icon. Having several of these in the Controls list could cause confusion (or just look boring).

To modify the custom control icon that is used for your template part, follow these steps:

1. With your form template part file open in InfoPath Designer, select File, Info to display the Form Information screen.

2. Click the Template Part Properties button to display the Template Part Properties dialog.

3. Click Browse to browse for a new picture file and click Open on the file dialog.

4. Click OK on the Template Part Properties dialog.

5. Click File, Save to save the changes to your form template part file.

NOTE You will need to remove the old template part custom control and add the new one to see the icon changes.

CHAPTER 15

Document Information Panel Content Type

The Document Information Panel (DIP) is a form that appears within a Microsoft Office application (Excel, PowerPoint, or Word) when you are creating a new document for a SharePoint document library that contains custom columns. The DIP allows you to enter additional information about the document and have those values stored in the SharePoint document library.

The DIP is actually part of the document content type used within the document library. Adding columns to your document library updates the DIP portion of the content type. Essentially, the DIP is an extension of the Excel, PowerPoint, or Word document itself.

InfoPath Designer has a Document Information Panel template available for when designing a new form. Although this might make you think you can create a new DIP, the option is actually there to modify an existing DIP. Because the DIP is part of the content type, it needs to be system generated within the document library first before any modifications can be made.

Create the Document Library

Scenario/Problem: You need to create a library to store Office documents that can use the DIP.

Solution: In SharePoint, create a new document library that uses a Microsoft Office document template.

Before you modify a DIP for your documents, you need a document library that stores the documents. The document template for the library needs to be one of the Microsoft Office document templates (Excel, PowerPoint, or Word), as shown in Figure 15.1.

FIGURE 15.1
Selecting a Microsoft Office template allows a DIP to be applied.

Add Columns to Your DIP

Scenario/Problem: You need to add the additional columns to be used in your DIP.

Solution: Modify the document library in SharePoint and add the additional columns.

Because the DIP is used to display/enter the additional data you want to capture with the documents, you need to have columns in your library to store those values.

To add these columns to your library, follow these steps:

1. Navigate to your document library in SharePoint.

2. Click Library Settings on the Library ribbon bar, as shown in Figure 15.2, to manage the library's settings.

FIGURE 15.2
Clicking Library Settings allows you to manage the library's settings.

3. On the List Information page, scroll down and click Create Column, as shown in Figure 15.3, to add a new column to the library.

4. Enter a name for the column and select the type of information. Click OK.

5. Repeat steps 1 and 2 for additional columns.

6. Navigate back to the document library.

7. From the Documents ribbon bar, select New Document, as shown in Figure 15.4, to launch the Microsoft Office application associated to the document library document type.

FIGURE 15.3
Clicking Create Column allows you to add new columns to your document library.

FIGURE 15.4
Clicking New Document launches the Office application associated to the document library

The Office application launches and displays a blank new document. The system-generated DIP appears at the top of the document, as shown in Figure 15.5. Verify that the DIP contains the additional columns you added to the library.

> **TIP**   If your DIP does not show by default, go to File | Info and click the Form
> Template Properties button on the far right. In the properties dialog click Show
> Document Panel.

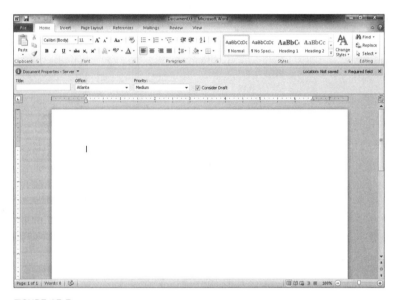

FIGURE 15.5
Creating a new document verifies that the added columns appear in the DIP.

> **NOTE**   Any multiple-choice columns are displayed as drop-downs regardless of the
> selection in SharePoint, but you may modify the control inside the DIP to use different
> interfaces.

Modify the DIP

> **Scenario/Problem:** You want to modify the system-generated DIP.

The first step in modifying a DIP is using the form template to create a new form to
modify the DIP. To modify the DIP of a document library, follow these steps:

1. From the File, New page, select the Document Information Panel template, as
   shown in Figure 15.6, to import an existing DIP for modification.

2. Click the Design Form button. The Data Source Wizard appears.

3. Enter the address of the document library for which you want to modify the DIP,
   as shown in Figure 15.7. Click Next.

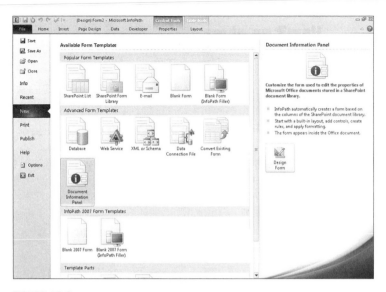

FIGURE 15.6
Selecting the Document Information Panel template allows you to import an existing DIP for modification.

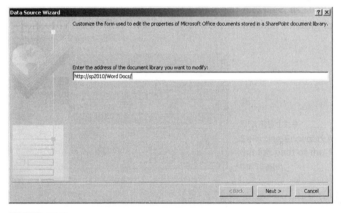

FIGURE 15.7
Entering the document library address determines which DIP to modify.

4. Select the content type in the library, as shown in Figure 15.8, to modify the DIP of that document type. Click Next.

5. Click Finish. The system-generated DIP for the document library content type you selected is loaded into the designer, as shown in Figure 15.9.

6. Modify the DIP inside the designer as needed.

7. Click File, Info, and then click the Quick Publish button to publish your changes to the document library. You need to save a local copy of the form before InfoPath allows you to publish the form.

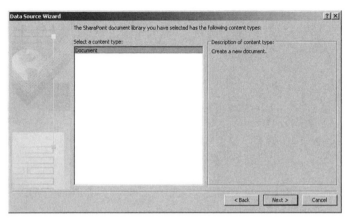

FIGURE 15.8
Selecting the content type modifies the DIP of that document type.

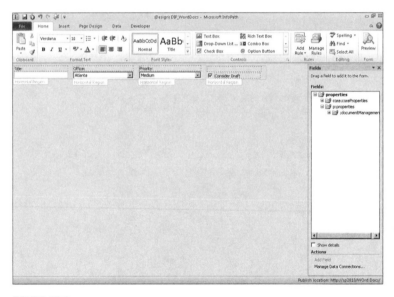

FIGURE 15.9
Clicking Finish loads the DIP into the designer.

Publishing the new template updates the document content type in the document library.

> **TIP** Add data connections to your DIP to populate drop-downs with dynamic data.

Adding a new document through the associated Office application renders your updated template as the document information panel.

CHAPTER 16

Leveraging Visual Studio 2010 with InfoPath

This chapter explores several ways to use Visual Studio 2010 with InfoPath. Visual Studio 2010 can be leveraged to create workflows for an InfoPath form as well as to create application-level add-ins.

The creation of Visual Studio workflows and the customization of Office products are broad subjects within themselves, and plenty of resources discuss these topics in great detail. The scenarios in this chapter provide a primer for using Visual Studio 2010 with InfoPath.

Access Your Form Within a Visual Studio Workflow

Scenario/Problem: You need to obtain the values entered into a form within a Visual Studio workflow.

Solution: Create a class based on your form and serialize an object.

You may access the form contents within a workflow by creating an object of the form. To create an object, you need to define a class that defines the structure of your form. Luckily, utilities are available to automatically generate this class for you.

First you need the source files of your InfoPath form. There are two ways to accomplish this. One way is to export the source files from InfoPath, and the other is to just extract them from your form template file.

To export the source files of your form, follow these steps:

1. Open your form in design mode using InfoPath Designer 2010.
2. Click File, Publish.
3. Click the Export Source Files button, as shown in Figure 16.1. The Browse for Folder dialog appears.
4. Select a folder location and click OK. The source files are saved to the folder selected.
5. Close InfoPath Designer.

TIP When creating a new folder to save the source files, it is a good idea to include Source Files in the name so you know what it contains (for example, Registration Form Source Files).

To extract the source files right from the form template, follow these steps:

1. Navigate to your form template in Windows Explorer.
2. Rename the form replacing .xsn with .cab.

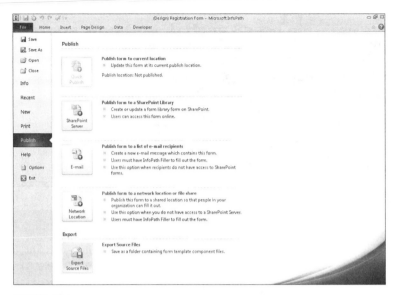

FIGURE 16.1
Clicking Export Source Files exports your form's source files to a folder.

3. Open the .cab file. The source files are there!

4. Select all of the source files.

5. Right-click and select Extract. The Select a Destination dialog appears.

6. Navigate to the folder where you want to save the files and click Extract. The source files are extracted to the location.

7. Rename the form back to .xsn.

The file that you are most interested in is the myschema.xsd file. This contains the XML definition of your form. Using the Visual Studio xsd.exe utility, you can easily generate a class file using myschema.xsd. To do this, follow these steps:

1. Open a Visual Studio command prompt. (This can be found under Start, Microsoft Visual Studio 2010, Visual Studio Tools.)

2. Navigate to the location of your form source files.

3. Type xsd /c myschema.xsd and press Enter, as shown in Figure 16.2.

NOTE   At the time of this writing, the xsd utility could not generate code for all InfoPath controls. If you run into any problems, search for any patches or updates.

4. Back in Windows Explorer, rename the .cs file that was generated to your form name (for example, RegistrationForm.cs).

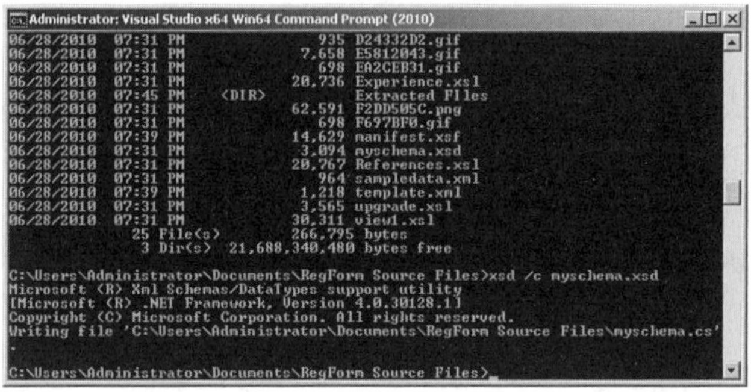

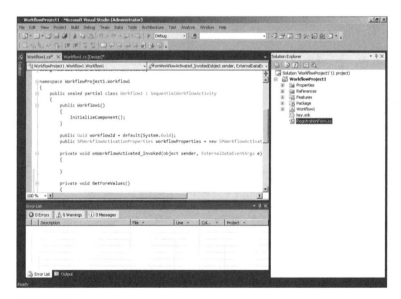

FIGURE 16.2
Using the xsd utility generates the class file.

5. Optionally, copy the .cs file into your workflow project folder.

6. Add the .cs file to your workflow project, as shown in Figure 16.3.

7. Copy the namespace from your workflow class file and paste it into your form class file, as shown in Figure 16.4. Your form classes must be in the same namespace to be accessed within the workflow code.

FIGURE 16.3
Adding the form .cs file to your project allows you to leverage the form class.

Now the class is part of the workflow project. The next steps and code pertain to the workflow class:

1. Open the workflow class file.

2. Add the proper using statements as listed in Listing 16.1 at the top of the class. Because access to the form is done through XML serialization, these references need to be made.

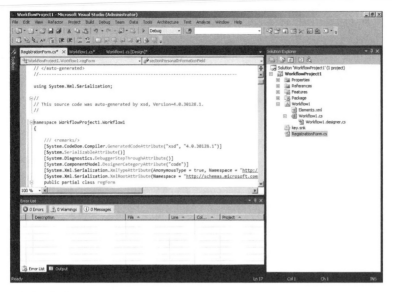

FIGURE 16.4
Placing the form classes into the workflow namespace allows you to access the objects within the workflow code.

3. Create a GetFormValues method, as shown in Listing 16.2.

> **NOTE** This example assumes that you did not modify the main data source name from myFields to something else, although it is a good idea to rename the main data source to the form name or similar.

LISTING 16.1 **Using Statements**

```
using System.Xml;
using System.Xml.Serialization;
```

LISTING 16.2 **GetFormValues**

```
private void GetFormValues()
{
    XmlSerializer serializer = new XmlSerializer(typeof(myFields));
    XmlTextReader reader = new XmlTextReader(new System.IO.StringReader
(workflowProperties.InitiationData));
    myFields registrationForm = (myFields)serializer.Deserialize(reader);
}
```

4. Call the GetFormValues() method from the onWorkflowActivated_Invoked method or anywhere else needed in your workflow code.

You may now access the form as an object and set class variables to the values the user entered, as shown in Figure 16.5.

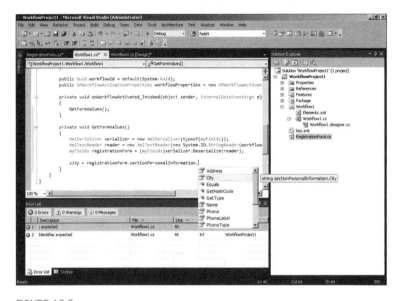

FIGURE 16.5
Serializing the object allows you to access the entered values.

Create an InfoPath 2010 Add-In

Scenario/Problem: You need to create an InfoPath 2010 add-in.

Solution: Use Visual Studio 2010 and create a new add-in project.

You may use Visual Studio 2010 to create an InfoPath 2010 add-in that can be used within InfoPath. The add-in is an application-level add-in that customizes the InfoPath Designer experience. Two common uses of an InfoPath add-in are to customize the ribbon and generate a custom task pane.

To create an InfoPath 2010 add-in, follow these steps:

1. Launch Visual Studio 2010.

2. Click File, New, Project. The New Project dialog appears.

3. Navigate to Office, 2010 from the left-side Installed Templates navigation.

4. Select the InfoPath 2010 Add-In project template, as shown in Figure 16.6.

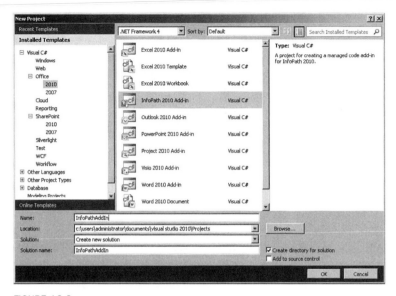

FIGURE 16.6
Selecting the project template generates an InfoPath 2010 add-in project.

5. Click OK.

6. Add user controls or classes as appropriate; see the next section for an example.

7. Build the add-in project. The add-in is generated.

8. Open InfoPath Designer 2010.

9. Click the COM Add-Ins button on the Developer ribbon. The add-in is available and installed, as shown in Figure 16.7

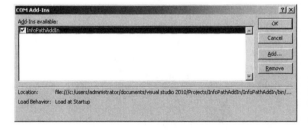

FIGURE 16.7
Clicking COM Add-Ins shows the available and installed application add-ins.

Create a Custom Task Pane

Scenario/Problem: You want to create a custom task pane.

Solution: Use Visual Studio 2010 to create a new InfoPath add-in.

To create a new task pane, follow the steps for creating a new InfoPath 2010 add-in. Then perform these steps:

1. Add a user control to your project.

2. Add windows controls to your user control as needed. In this example, a user control named CustomTaskPaneControl is used.

3. Add any code to handle options or selections.

4. In the ThisAddIn class, add private variables to handle the user control and custom task pane, as shown in Listing 16.3.

5. In the startup method of the ThisAddIn class, add code to instantiate the user control as a custom task pane, as shown in Listing 16.4.

LISTING 16.3 **Private Declarations**

```
private CustomTaskPaneControl customTaskPaneControl;

private Microsoft.Office.Tools.CustomTaskPane customTaskPane;
```

LISTING 16.4 **Custom Task Pane Instantiation**

```
customTaskPaneControl = new CustomTaskPaneControl();
customTaskPane = this.CustomTaskPanes.Add(customTaskPaneControl, "Custom
Task Pane");

customTaskPane.Visible = true;
```

6. Build the project, and then launch InfoPath Designer 2010. The custom task pane appears as shown in Figure 16.8.

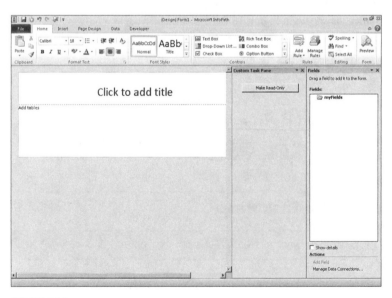

FIGURE 16.8
Building a custom task pane add-in displays the user control in InfoPath.

CHAPTER 17

Dynamically Populate a Repeating Table

This chapter covers the steps necessary to dynamically populate a repeating table. Displaying data from a data source in a repeating table is fairly straightforward using rules and filters. However, in this overall scenario, you need to populate a repeating group in your form with data from a data source. The data is dependent on another selection in your form.

Changing the selection in the form queries the data source based on that selection and populates a repeating table with the data. If the selection changes, the repeating table entries need to be cleared and repopulated with the new set of data.

To clarify the data sources, the external data source is a secondary data source, and the repeating table is bound as a repeating group of fields in the main data source.

Set Up the Initial Form

Scenario/Problem: You need to set up the initial form.

Solution: The initial form contains at least a selection field and a repeating group of fields to populate. The selection field can be populated by a data source if required. A secondary data source exists to populate the repeating table.

To set up the initial form, follow these steps:

1. Design a new form in InfoPath Designer 2010.

2. Add a drop-down list control to the form and name the field accordingly. (For the example, I used Selection.)

3. Add a repeating table to the form, selecting the number of columns as appropriate. Rename the fields accordingly. For this example, I kept the default of three columns and renamed only the repeating group to groupRepeat. Your form should now look similar to Figure 17.1.

4. Add a data connection to retrieve data for the selection field. Modify the selection field accordingly. For this example, I am retrieving Regions from a SharePoint list.

5. Add a data connection to retrieve data for the population of the repeating table; let's call this the dependent data source. For this example, I am retrieving Offices from a SharePoint list.

6. Add a rule on the selection field such that when the selection changes you set the query field and query the dependent data source that you will use to populate the repeating table. For this example, I set the Region query field of the Offices data source to the selection field, as shown in Figure 17.2, to retrieve the related data.

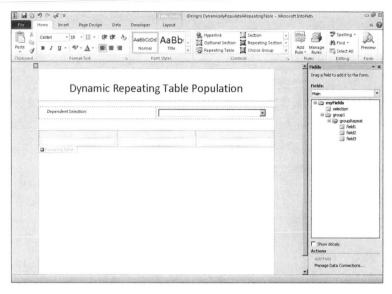

FIGURE 17.1
Adding the controls to the form performs the initial form setup.

7. For testing purposes, drag the repeating group of the dependent data source onto the form.

8. Preview the form and ensure that changing the selection changes the data source repeating table, as shown in Figure 17.3.

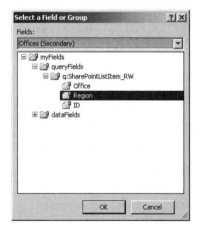

FIGURE 17.2
Setting the query field value retrieves the related data.

So now the challenge is to place those entries of the dependent data source into the repeating table of the form.

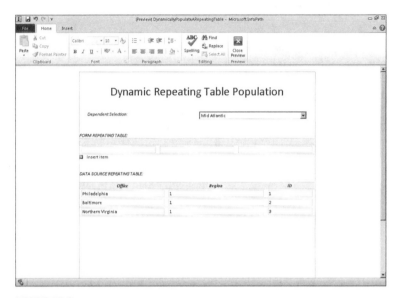

FIGURE 17.3
Changing the selection field changes the data source repeating table.

Create a Changed Event Method

Scenario/Problem: You need to create a changed event method on a control.

Solution: Select the control and click the Changed Event button on the Developer ribbon bar.

Creating any methods produces code-behind in your form. For the overall scenario of this chapter, you need to generate a changed event method and place the code within that method.

For the example, select the drop-down list control and then click the Changed Event button on the Developer ribbon bar to generate the code-behind method, as shown in Figure 17.4.

NOTE   To use code-behind, you need Microsoft Office Visual Studio Tools for Applications (VSTA) installed. If you do not have this installed, you may change the Microsoft InfoPath 2010 program in the Control Panel and select the VSTA option under Microsoft Office, Microsoft InfoPath, .NET Programmability Support.

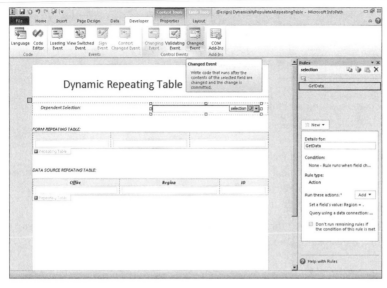

FIGURE 17.4
Clicking Changed Event generates the code-behind method.

The code is generated with an event handler declaration and a blank changed method, as shown in Figure 17.5.

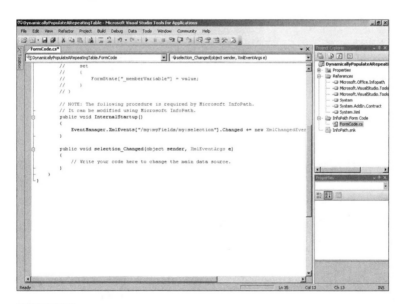

FIGURE 17.5
Generating the code produces the event handler and changed method.

Create a Namespace Variable

Scenario/Problem: You need to create a namespace variable.

Solution: Declare a string variable and set that to the namespace using the NamespaceManager object.

Coding with InfoPath involves using XML/XPath objects and methods as well as XPath expressions. A key element in using the XML/XPath methods is the namespace that is used for the XML data retrieval. The `NamespaceManager` object enables you to look up the namespace. By default, the namespace in InfoPath data is my.

Because the namespace is used throughout various methods in this solution, the first line of code in the changed method is a string variable declaration, as shown in Listing 17.1.

LISTING 17.1 **Namespace Declaration**

```
//Namespace variable
string myNamespace = NamespaceManager.LookupNamespace("my");
```

Access the Secondary Data Source

Scenario/Problem: You need to access the secondary data source.

Solution: Create DataSource and XPath objects using the secondary data source information.

The next step in the overall solution is to declare objects based on the secondary data source. You need the name of the secondary data source and the XPath of the rows that are returned. To retrieve the XPath of the rows returned, follow these steps:

1. Switch over to your InfoPath form.
2. In the Fields pane, switch the data source to the secondary data source. (For this example, it is Offices.)
3. Expand the datafields folder.
4. Right-click the repeating group under the datafields folder and select Copy XPath to copy the XPath string to the Clipboard, as shown in Figure 17.6.
5. Switch back to the code-behind and paste the XPath into the code as needed.

The secondary data source setup code is shown in Listing 17.2. Paste the XPath from the previous steps into the `XPathNavigator Select` method. Place this block of code after the namespace variable.

LISTING 17.2 **Secondary Data Source Setup**

```
//Secondary data source setup
DataSource ds = DataSources["OFFICES"];
XPathNavigator domNav = ds.CreateNavigator();
XPathNodeIterator rows = domNav.Select
("/dfs:myFields/dfs:dataFields/d:SharePointListItem_RW",
NamespaceManager);
```

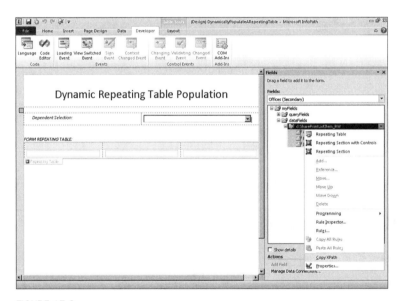

FIGURE 17.6
Selecting Copy XPath places the XPath string into the Clipboard.

Loop Through the Secondary Data Source

Scenario/Problem: You need to loop through the secondary data source.

Solution: Create a while loop to loop through the rows.

The loop is the main component of populating the repeating table. You loop through the secondary data source through the XPathNodeIterator collection (rows) that you defined in the previous section, retrieving the values from each row. The code to perform this is shown in Listing 17.3. Place this after the secondary data source setup. You will add more code to the loop in the next section.

> **TIP**   Check the XPath of the secondary data source fields to determine how to call reference their nodes.

LISTING 17.3 **Loop Through the Secondary Data Source**

```
//Loop through the secondary data source
while (rows.MoveNext())
{
string office = rows.Current.SelectSingleNode("D:TITLE",
NamespaceManager).Value.ToString();
    string region = rows.Current.SelectSingleNode("D:REGION",
NamespaceManager).Value.ToString();
    string id = rows.Current.SelectSingleNode("D:ID",
 NamespaceManager).Value.ToString();

}
```

> **NOTE**   The variables defined in the loop should correspond to the fields that are returned from the secondary data source.

Populate the Repeating Table

> **Scenario/Problem:** You need to populate the repeating table.

Solution: Use the XMLWriter to write the values from the secondary data source to the repeating group in the form.

The repeating table is actually part of the main data source, so you can access that and use the XMLWriter to write the field values from the secondary data source to the table.

You will need the names of the groups and the fields that are bound to the repeating table in the form. In this example, the groups are group1 and groupRepeat, and the fields are field1, field2, and field3.

Place the code in Listing 17.4 within the while loop from the preceding section.

> **TIP** Copy the XPath from the repeating group to ensure the correct path is entered.

LISTING 17.4 **Populate the Repeating Table**

```
//Populate the repeating table
using (XmlWriter writer = MainDataSource.CreateNavigator().SelectSingle-
Node("/my:myFields/my:group1", NamespaceManager).AppendChild())
{
    writer.WriteStartElement("groupRepeat", myNamespace);
    writer.WriteElementString("field1",myNamespace,office);
    writer.WriteElementString("field2", myNamespace,region);
    writer.WriteElementString("field3", myNamespace,id);
    writer.WriteEndElement();
    writer.Close();
}
```

> **NOTE**   The order in which you write the values to the table should be the order
> that they appear in the main data source. Otherwise, you will receive a non-datatype
> schema validation error.

Clear Previous Entries

> **Scenario/Problem:** You need to clear previous entries.

Solution: Loop through the repeating table and clear the values.

If you preview the form at this point, you will notice that every time you select a value
from the selection drop-down, the repeating table is populated with more and more
entries (along with a blank row at the top). You therefore need to clear any previous
entries before the repeating table is populated. Place the code listed in Listing 17.4
somewhere before the while loop.

LISTING 17.4 **Clear Previous Entries**

```
//Clear previous entries
XPathNavigator rTable = MainDataSource.CreateNavigator();
XPathNodeIterator tableRows =
rTable.Select("/my:myFields/my:group1/my:groupRepeat",
NamespaceManager);
if (tableRows.Count > 0)
{
```

LISTING 17.4 **Clear Previous Entries** (continued)

```
  for (int i = tableRows.Count; i > 0; i--)
  {
    XPathNavigator reTable = MainDataSource.CreateNavigator();
    XPathNavigator reTableRows =
reTable.SelectSingleNode("/my:myFields/my:group1/my:groupRepeat[" + i
 + "]", NamespaceManager);
    reTableRows.DeleteSelf();
  }
}
```

What Does the Final Solution Look Like?

When all the code has been entered into the method properly, previewing the form populates the repeating table based on the selection in the drop-down, as shown in Figure 17.7.

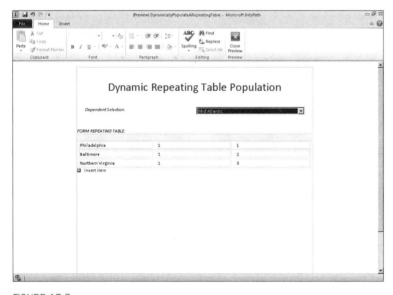

FIGURE 17.7
Changing the selection populates the repeating table.

Listing 17.5 shows the full code listing for the changed method.

LISTING 17.5 **Fully Changed Method**

```
public void selection_Changed(object sender, XmlEventArgs e)
        {

            //Namespace variable
            string myNamespace = NamespaceManager.LookupNamespace("my");

            //Clear previous entries
            XPathNavigator rTable = MainDataSource.CreateNavigator();
    XPathNodeIterator tableRows =
rTable.Select("/my:myFields/my:group1/my:groupRepeat",
NamespaceManager);
            if (tableRows.Count > 0)
            {

                for (int i = tableRows.Count; i > 0; i--)
                {
                    XPathNavigator reTable =
                    MainDataSource.CreateNavigator();
                    XPathNavigator reTableRows =

                    reTable.SelectSingleNode
("/my:myFields/my:group1/my:groupRepeat[" + i + "]",
NamespaceManager);
                    reTableRows.DeleteSelf();
                }
            }

            //Secondary data source setup
            DataSource ds = DataSources["Offices"];
            XPathNavigator domNav = ds.CreateNavigator();
            XPathNodeIterator rows = domNav.Select("/dfs:myFields/
dfs:dataFields/d:SharePointListItem_RW", NamespaceManager);


            //Loop through the secondary data source
            while (rows.MoveNext())
            {
                string office =
rows.Current.SelectSingleNode("d:Title",
NamespaceManager).Value.ToString();
                string region = rows.Current.SelectSingleNode("d:Region",
NamespaceManager).Value.ToString();
                string id =
```

LISTING 17.5 **Fully Changed Method** (continued)

```
rows.Current.SelectSingleNode("d:ID",
NamespaceManager).Value.ToString();

            //Populate the repeating table
            using (XmlWriter writer =

MainDataource.CreateNavigator().SelectSingleNode("/my:myFields/
my:group1", NamespaceManager).AppendChild())
        {
            writer.WriteStartElement("groupRepeat", myNamespace);
            writer.WriteElementString("field1", myNamespace, office);
            writer.WriteElementString("field2", myNamespace, region);
            writer.WriteElementString("field3", myNamespace, id);
            writer.WriteEndElement();
            writer.Close();
        }

            }

        }
```

CHAPTER 18

Track Changes in a Form

This chapter is dedicated to a code-behind solution that allows the tracking of changes within a SharePoint form. Many times, forms are used in workflows where many different people may access and edit the form contents. During this process, the business may want to see what changed as the form is passed onto the next group or responsible party.

There is no out-of-the-box functionality for tracking changes in InfoPath, but with the proper controls, rules, and code-behind, you can implement a great solution.

Set Up the Form for Tracking Changes

Scenario/Problem: You want to set up the form for tracking changes.

Solution: Create the controls and fields needed for tracking changes as explained here.

The initial setup starts with defining the field and text box for the form entry you want to track changes.

To define the field and text box, follow these steps:

1. Design a new form in InfoPath Designer and use a single-column table layout.

2. Place a text box in the second row and provide a name for the field. (For this example, I am using Description.) This is the field for which you want to track changes.

3. Make the text box multiline and stretch it out within the table row.

4. Split the cells of the first row and enter a field label in the first column.

5. Make the second column smaller by dragging the line that separates the two columns. The second column will be used for controls as explained within subsequent sections.

Your form should now look similar to Figure 18.1.

The next steps for the initial setup are to provide the storage for the changes being made to the field:

1. Drag a repeating section under the text box you added in the previous steps.

2. Modify the properties of the repeating section and uncheck the Allow Users to Insert or Delete the Sections option.

3. In the Fields pane, rename the first group to groupTrackChanges.

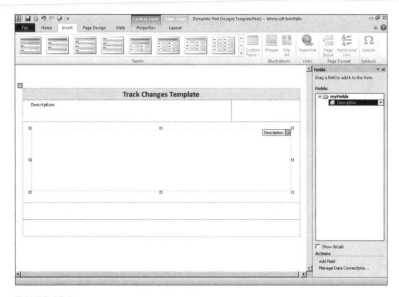

FIGURE 18.1
The multiline text box is the field in which InfoPath will track changes.

4. Rename the repeating group2 to groupChanges.

5. Under the groupChanges, add a field named NumberOfChanges and make its data type a Whole Number (Integer).

6. Under the groupChanges, add a field named Changes and make its data type Rich Text (XHTML).

7. Under the groupChanges, add a field named UserName and leave its data type as Text (String).

8. Drag the Changes field into the repeating section on the form.

9. Resize the rich text box such that it is the same as the normal text box and make it read-only.

Your form should now look similar to Figure 18.2.

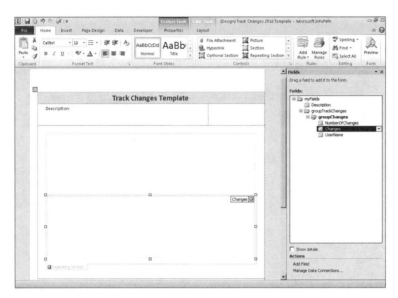

FIGURE 18.2
The repeating group will contain the changes made to in the text box.

Add Changed Event Code for Tracking Changes

Scenario/Problem: You need to add changed event code for tracking changes to your field.

Solution: Select the field and click Changed Event on the Developer ribbon.

The next step for tracking changes is to add the code-behind to facilitate the storing of the changes. The code executes when the text in the text boxes changes. To add the code-behind, follow these steps:

1. Select the field (Description in the example) on the form.

2. On the Developer ribbon, click Changed Event. The Code Editor appears.

3. Add the Microsoft.SharePoint assembly as a reference to the project, as shown in Figure 18.3. This allows you to access a special difference utility.

4. Add System.Web as a reference such that the HTTP Context may be used.

5. Add the proper using statements at the top of the FormCode.cs to reference the SharePoint utility and System.Web, as shown in Listing 18.1.

6. In the Changed method, add a string declaration for the namespace and the username, as shown in Listing 18.2

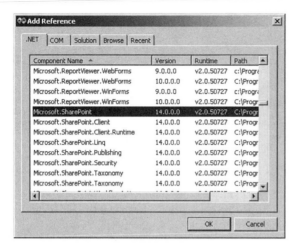

FIGURE 18.3
Adding a reference to SharePoint allows you to access a special difference utility.

7. Populate the `userName` variable with the current user filling out the form by using the HTTP context (Listing 18.3).

8. Declare color variables for the types of changes as shown in Listing 18.4. The color codes are HTML-based color codes.

LISTING 18.1 **Using References**

```
using Microsoft.SharePoint;
using Microsoft.SharePoint.Utilities;
using System.Web;
```

LISTING 18.2 **String Declarations**

```
//Get namespace
string myNamespace = NamespaceManager.LookupNamespace("MY");
string userName = string.Empty;
```

LISTING 18.3 **Populate userName**

```
if (HttpContext.Current != null)
{
    userName = HttpContext.Current.User.Identity.Name.ToString();
}
```

LISTING 18.4 **Color Variable Declarations**

```
//Color Variables
string changeColor = "#330066";
string deleteColor = "#FF0000";
string insertColor = "#008000";
```

> **TIP** Declare the color variables as constants if you are tracking changes on multiple text boxes.

You will now use the SPDiffUtility provided by the SharePoint assembly to produce the track changes results. This is facilitated by setting up the Open and Close tags using HTML strings and then calling the Diff method from the utility. This code is shown in Listing 18.5. At this point, your changed method should look similar to Figure 18.4.

LISTING 18.5 **SPDiffUtility Code**

```
//Set the tags
SPDiffUtility.ChangeOpenTag = "<FONT COLOR="" + changeColor + ""
xmlns="http://www.w3.org/1999/xhtml">";
SPDiffUtility.ChangeCloseTag = "</FONT>";
SPDiffUtility.DeleteOpenTag = "<STRIKE XMLNS="HTTP://WWW.W3.ORG/1999/
XHTML"><FONT COLOR="" + deleteColor
 + "">";
SPDiffUtility.DeleteCloseTag = "</FONT></STRIKE>";
SPDiffUtility.InsertOpenTag = "<FONT COLOR="" + insertColor + ""
xmlns="http://www.w3.org/1999/xhtml">";
SPDiffUtility.InsertCloseTag = "</FONT>";

//Get the changes
string newValue = SPDiffUtility.Diff(e.OldValue, e.NewValue, 255);
```

Now you need to apply the new value to your form, which involves adding it to the repeating group. Add the code from Listing 18.6 to your method to facilitate this.

The NumberOfChanges gets set to the number of rows, the Changes field takes the changes from the SPDiffUtility, and the UserName gets set to the user making the changes.

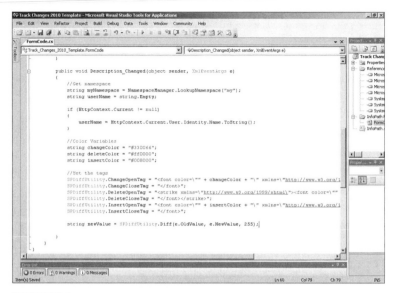

FIGURE 18.4
The SPDiffUtility produces the changed values based on the configured tags.

LISTING 18.6 **Create a New Entry**

```
//Create New Entry
XPathNavigator rTable = MainDataSource.CreateNavigator();
XPathNodeIterator tableRows = rTable.Select("/MY:MYFIELDS/
MY:GROUPTRACKCHANGES/MY:GROUPCHANGES",
NamespaceManager);
string rowNumber = Convert.ToString(tableRows.Count + 1);

using (XmlWriter writer = MainDataSource.CreateNavigator()
.SelectSingleNode("/MY:MYFIELDS/MY:GROUPTRACKCHANGES",
NamespaceManager).AppendChild())
{
writer.WriteStartElement("GROUPCHANGES", myNamespace);
   writer.WriteElementString("NUMBEROFCHANGES", myNamespace,
rowNumber);
   writer.WriteElementString("CHANGES", myNamespace, newValue);
   writer.WriteElementString("USERNAME", myNamespace, userName);

   writer.WriteEndElement();
   writer.Close();
}
```

> **TIP** Make sure you write the elements in the same order as they appear in your repeating group.

Before you preview the form, you need to change the security of the form:

1. Select File, Info.

2. Click the Form Options button. The Form Options dialog appears.

3. In the Form Options dialog, select Security and Trust.

4. Change the security level to Full Trust, as shown in Figure 18.5.

5. Click OK.

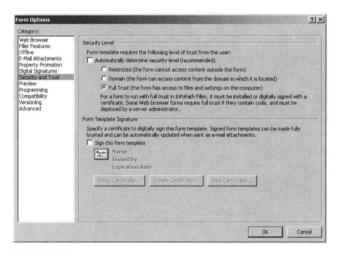

FIGURE 18.5
Changing the security allows the code to execute in the form.

Preview your form and add some text into the first text box. Click anywhere outside of the text box to trigger the change. The repeating section gets a new entry, as shown in Figure 18.6. The entry shows the HTML and not the rich text. The next section shows you how to apply rich text to the entry.

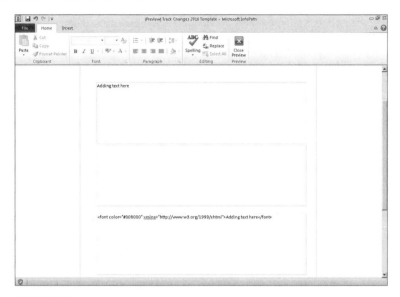

FIGURE 18.6
Adding text to the text box produces a new entry in the repeating section.

Apply Rich Text to the Entry

Scenario/Problem: Following the procedures in the previous sections produces the change HTML but does not apply rich text formatting to the entry. You therefore need to apply rich text formatting to the entry.

Solution: Add code to append the Changes value.

The last section of code in the method creates the new entry, but the Changes field contains only text. For the rich text to appear, the value needs to be appended to the Changes field. Add the code in Listing 18.7 to the bottom of your method.

LISTING 18.7 **Apply Rich Text**

```
//Apply Rich Text to new Element
XPathNavigator repTable = MainDataSource.CreateNavigator();
XPathNodeIterator repTableRows = repTable.Select("/MY:MYFIELDS/
MY:GROUPTRACKCHANGES/MY:GROUPCHANGES", NamespaceManager);
if (repTableRows.Count > 0)
{
    int i = repTableRows.Count;
    repTable.SelectSingleNode
```

LISTING 18.7 **Apply Rich Text** (continued)

```
("/MY:MYFIELDS/MY:GROUPTRACKCHANGES/MY:GROUPCHANGES[" + i +
"]/MY:CHANGES", NamespaceManager).SetValue("");
  repTable.SelectSingleNode
("/MY:MYFIELDS/MY:GROUPTRACKCHANGES/MY:GROUPCHANGES[" + i +
"]/MY:CHANGES", NamespaceManager).AppendChild(newValue);
}
```

The code now produces the desired rich text within the rich text boxes, as shown in Figure 18.7.

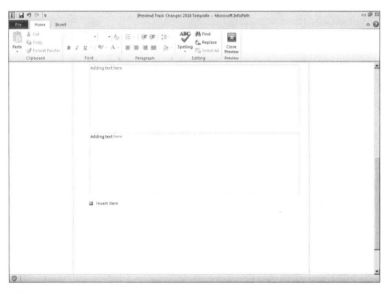

FIGURE 18.7
Appending the value produces the desired rich text.

Only Show One Version at a Time

Scenario/Problem: The current solution displays the entered text and all the changes. You want to show only one version of the text at a time.

Solution: Create navigation controls and add formatting rules accordingly.

It is now time to clean up the form such that only one text box is showing at a time. First you need a field to keep a pointer of which version is being shown and add rules to hide the controls:

1. Create a new field under myFields named ViewChanges with a data type of Whole Number (Integer) and a default value of –1.

2. Add a formatting rule on the groupChanges such that when the NumberOfChanges field is not equal to the ViewChanges field value, hide the control. This enables you to show only the entry that is being viewed. An example is shown in Figure 18.8.

3. Add a formatting rule on the original field (Description) to hide the control when ViewChanges is less than or equal to the maximum NumberOfChanges and ViewChanges is not equal to –1 (the default value), as shown in Figure 18.9. This determines when the text box is displayed.

> **TIP** You will need to use a formula for the maximum number of changes.

FIGURE 18.8
Adding the formatting rule hides any entries that are not being viewed.

The next set of steps produces the housing for the navigation controls:

1. Add a new section control to the second column of the first row.

2. Add a formatting rule to the section such that the control is hidden if ViewChanges is less than 2.

3. Insert a Two Column 3-table layout into the section.

4. Change the subheading to Change History.

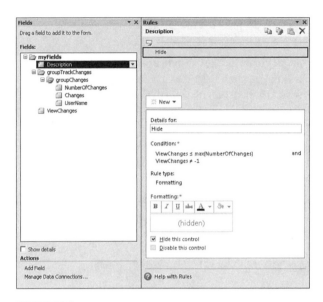

FIGURE 18.9
Adding the formatting rule determines when the text box is displayed.

5. Select the first column in the first row. Right-click and select split cells. Click OK on the Split Cells dialog.

6. Select the entire middle row. Right-click and select Merge Cells.

7. Remove the last row. Your section control should look similar to Figure 18.10.

> **TIP**   Change the padding of the cell to allow the new section to take up most of the cell space.

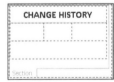

FIGURE 18.10
Configuring the table layout produces the housing for the navigation controls.

Now you need to produce navigation controls to increment or decrement the ViewChanges value. To do this, follow these steps:

1. In the Change History section control, add three picture buttons (one in each column that was split in the previous set of steps).

2. Add pictures to each button. The first one is a Previous button, the second one is a Next button, and the third one is an Edit button.

TIP SharePoint has many images located in C:Program FilesCommon FilesMicrosoft SharedWeb Server Extensions14TEMPLATEIMAGES on any server that has SharePoint installed. You can find standard icons for your picture buttons there!

3. Add an action rule to the Previous button to set ViewChanges equal to ViewChanges −1, as shown in Figure 18.11.

4. Add another action rule to the Previous button that sets the ViewChanges value to 2 based on the condition that ViewChanges is less than 2, as shown in Figure 18.12. Because there is a blank row that is automatically entered in the repeating group upon form rendering, you want to stop at 2 such that the blank row is not shown.

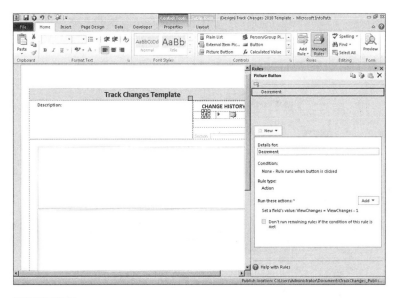

FIGURE 18.11
Adding the rule decrements the ViewChanges value when the button is clicked.

5. Add an action rule to the Next button to increment ViewChanges by 1.

6. Add an action rule to the Edit button setting the ViewChanges value equal to the maximum NumberOfChanges value + 1. You will need to use a formula as shown in Figure 18.13. Setting this value greater than the number of changes enables the field text box to display (based on the previous rules added to the text box).

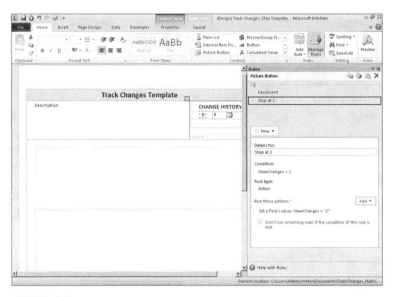

FIGURE 18.12
Adding the stop rule makes sure that the ViewChanges value doesn't become less than 2.

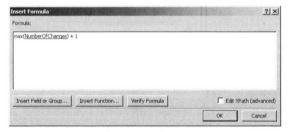

FIGURE 18.13
Setting ViewChanges greater than the number of changes displays the field text box.

TIP Add formatting rules to the picture buttons to disable the controls when they are not applicable.

You may optionally drag the ViewChanges field onto your form for debugging purposes. Previewing your form shows one text box at a time. Using the buttons navigates through the previous changes, as shown in Figure 18.14.

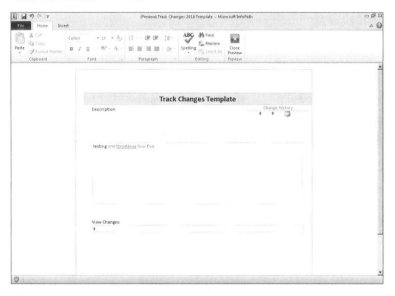

FIGURE 18.14
Using the buttons navigates through the changes.

Display a Changes Counter

Scenario/Problem: The current solution does not provide any indication of the current change.

Solution: Add a field to the Navigation Control section to display the change number.

While navigating through the changes, it helps users to understand where they are in relation to the changes. To provide this functionality, follow these steps:

1. Drag a text box onto the second row of the Change History section.

2. Rename the field to DisplayChangesCounter.

3. Set the default value equal to the concatenation of ViewChanges-1, the word "of" with padded spaces, and the maximum NumberOfChanges value, as shown in Figure 18.15, to produce the change counter display.

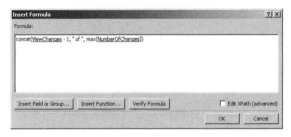

FIGURE 18.15
Concatenating the values produces the change counter display.

Previewing your form now displays the change counter information, as shown in Figure 18.16, alerting users of the current change they are viewing.

FIGURE 18.16
The change counter alerts the user of the current change that is being viewed.

> **TIP** To enhance the interface, make the DisplayChangesCounter text box read-only and remove any borders or shading. Change the alignment of the text to Center.

Display the User Who Made the Modification

> **Scenario/Problem:** You need to display the user who made the modification.

Solution: Add a field to the form that displays the username of the current entry of the repeating group.

While navigating through the changes, it helps users to understand who made the change that they are reviewing. To provide this functionality, follow these steps:

1. Drag a text box above the Description text box in main table row.

2. Name the field userName.

3. Make the text box read-only with no borders or shading.

4. Set the value of the text box equal to the value of the UserName field in the repeating group.

5. Before clicking OK, click the Filter Data button and add the filter condition of the NumberOfChanges is equal to ViewChanges, as shown in Figure 18.17. This allows only the UserName of the current entry to be displayed.

6. Add a formatting rule on the text box such that it is hidden if ViewChanges is less than 2.

FIGURE 18.17
Filtering the data allows the current user name to be displayed.

That's it! You will need to publish the form as an administrator-approved form and upload the form template to InfoPath Forms Services. (See Chapter 19, "Central Administration," or Chapter 20, "PowerShell," for more information about deploying administrator-approved forms.)

NOTE   Because the HTTP Context is being utilized to provide the username, you cannot preview this change. You will need to deploy the form to test the username implementation.

When deployed, open a new instance of your form. Cycling through the changes displays the associated username, as shown in Figure 18.18.

TIP   You may need another field on your form to click into such that the change code executes. Otherwise, clicking Close and then Cancel will cause the change to be recognized.

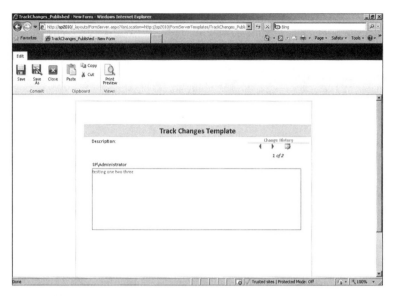

FIGURE 18.18
Cycling through the changes displays the user who made the change.

TIP Instead of tracking every change, you can place the same code into a different method (or remove the event handler statement in the InternalStartup() method) and call the method on the submission of your form to track only the submitted changes.

CHAPTER 19

Central Administration

IN THIS CHAPTER

This chapter dives into the administrative aspects of InfoPath Form Services using SharePoint 2010 Central Administration. SharePoint 2010 Central Administration is used to administer forms and Forms Services within your SharePoint farm.

Access the InfoPath Form Services Options

Scenario/Problem: You need to access the InfoPath Form Services options in Central Administration.

Solution: Launch Central Administration on one of the farm servers and select General Application Settings.

On one of the servers in your SharePoint farm, launch SharePoint 2010 Central Administration. A link is provided from the Start menu under All Programs, Microsoft SharePoint 2010 Products.

In Central Administration, click the General Application Settings link from the quick launch on the left side. The InfoPath Form Services options are located on that page, as shown in Figure 19.1.

FIGURE 19.1
The InfoPath Form Services options allow you to modify the settings of your SharePoint farm.

Browser-Enable Form Templates

Scenario/Problem: You need to allow custom SharePoint forms to be rendered within SharePoint.

Solution: Ensure the browser-enabled settings are selected under Configure InfoPath Form Services.

From Central Administration, General Application Settings, click the Configure InfoPath Form Services link under the InfoPath Form Services section. Make sure the first two check boxes are checked at the top of the page, as shown in Figure 19.2.

FIGURE 19.2
Checking the browser-enabled options allows SharePoint forms to be published and rendered on your farm.

The first selection allows browser-enabled forms to be published to SharePoint, and the second selection allows those forms to be rendered through the web browser.

Throttle Data Connection Timeouts

Scenario/Problem: You need to increase or decrease the data connection timeout limit.

Solution: Enter the default and maximum timeout values within Configure InfoPath Form Services.

Your form will attempt to connect and access data sources based on your configured data connections. If the data source is not accessible, busy, or down, InfoPath Forms Services needs a way to time out the connection such that the form or the browser doesn't stop responding.

From Central Administration, General Application Settings, click the Configure InfoPath Form Services link under the InfoPath Form Services section. Under the Data Connection Timeouts section, increase or decrease the values, as shown in Figure 19.3.

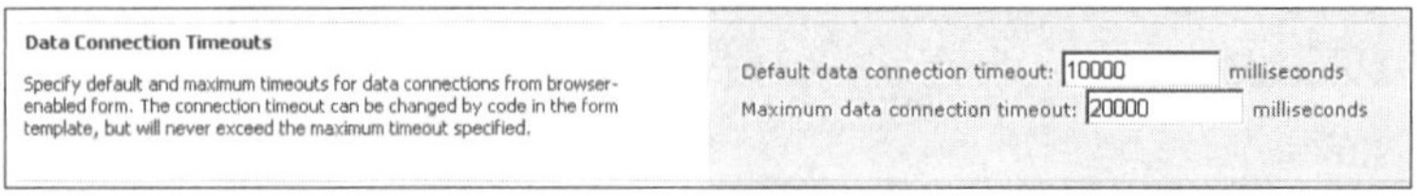

Data Connection Timeouts

Specify default and maximum timeouts for data connections from browser-enabled form. The connection timeout can be changed by code in the form template, but will never exceed the maximum timeout specified.

Default data connection timeout: 10000 milliseconds
Maximum data connection timeout: 20000 milliseconds

FIGURE 19.3
The data connection timeout values you set determine how long InfoPath waits for data activity.

TIP The default values are usually acceptable entries and do not need to be modified. However, if you have some long-running data processes or connectivity issues, you might want to increase these numbers slightly.

Throttle the Data Connection Response Size

Scenario/Problem: You need to increase or decrease the data connection response size.

Solution: Enter maximum response size value (in kilobytes) within Configure InfoPath Form Services.

When connecting to data sources, you do not want to overload other systems. Limiting the response size determines how many kilobytes the data connection can process.

From Central Administration, General Application Settings, click the Configure InfoPath Form Services link under the InfoPath Form Services section. Under the Data

Connection Response Size section, increase or decrease the values, as shown in Figure 19.4.

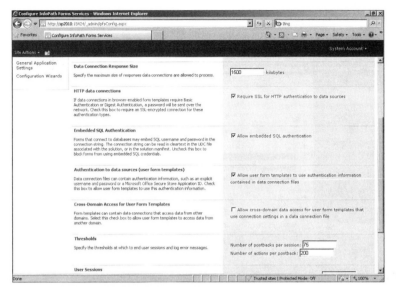

FIGURE 19.4
The response size value you set determines how many kilobytes the data connection can process.

> **TIP** The default value of 1500KB is usually a good setting. You do not want to strain other systems or databases. This also helps limit traffic on the network. Only increase this value if you have a large form that submits a great deal of data.

Modify Authentication Settings

> **Scenario/Problem:** You need to modify authentication settings.

Solution: Check or uncheck the authentication settings in Configure InfoPath Form Services.

Several data authentication options are available that either allow or prohibit certain types of data connectivity, including the following:

- ▶ **HTTP Data Connections:** Select this option to require SSL encryption when your form uses HTTP authentication (such as when accessing a web service).

- ▶ **Embedded SQL Authentication:** Select this option if you have data connection files that contain SQL database connection information, including the username and password.

▶ **Authentication to Data Sources:** Select this option to allow custom forms to access data sources through data connection files.

▶ **Cross-Domain Access:** Select this option if your form needs to access data sources on a different domain than SharePoint.

To configure these settings, from Central Administration, General Application Settings, click the Configure InfoPath Form Services link under the InfoPath Form Services section. Under the authentication sections, check or uncheck the options, as shown in Figure 19.5.

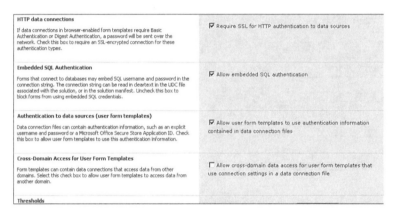

FIGURE 19.5
Checking the authentication options permits InfoPath to use various types of data connections.

Configure Session State

Scenario/Problem: You need to configure session state settings.

Solution: Modify the session state settings in Configure InfoPath Form Services.

When a user is filling out a SharePoint form, Form Services uses the SharePoint Server State service to manage user sessions. Transient data is stored within the session state.

Several settings are involved in the session state configuration:

▶ **Number of Postbacks per Session:** Typically, there shouldn't be too much chatter between the form and InfoPath Forms Services. This setting prevents unintended postbacks or "out-of-control" communications.

▶ **Number of Actions per Postback:** There should only be a handful of actions per postback. Once again, this is prevent a form process from pegging server resources.

▶ **Active Session Duration:** By default, active sessions are terminated after 1,440 minutes, which essentially is 24 hours. This is more of a cleanup process than anything. Some forms may take a long time to fill out depending on the information required, but one day should be plenty of time.

▶ **Maximum Size of User Session Data:** This determines how much data can be stored for the active user session. The default is 4096KB, which equates to 4MB. This provides plenty of room to store user session data. Typical forms and user information should take up only several kilobytes if not bytes.

If the user session lasts too long or there too many postbacks to the server, the session is ended based on the configured settings. All form data will be lost, and the user will need to start over. This is done to prevent unintended communication, limit network traffic, and limit system resource utilization.

To configure these settings, from Central Administration, General Application Settings, click the Configure InfoPath Form Services link under the InfoPath Form Services section. Under the Thresholds and User Sessions sections, modify the values, as shown in Figure 19.6.

Thresholds	
Specify the thresholds at which to end user sessions and log error messages.	Number of postbacks per session: 75
	Number of actions per postback: 200

User Sessions	
Specify time and data limits for user sessions. User session data is stored by the Microsoft SharePoint Server State Service.	Active sessions should be terminated after: 1440 minutes
	Maximum size of user session data: 4096 kilobytes

FIGURE 19.6
Modifying the thresholds and user session values configures the session state.

> **TIP** If forms are constantly being filled out within your organization and are fairly lightweight, you may actually want to reduce some of these values to keep recycling the session state as well as system resources. Another option is to use view state instead, which is available only to configure using PowerShell. See Chapter 20, "PowerShell," for more information about enabling view state using PowerShell.

Upload a Form Template

> **Scenario/Problem:** You need to upload a form template to InfoPath Form Services.

Solution: Click the Upload Form Template link under the InfoPath Form Services section.

Forms that have code-behind or that require full trust cannot be published directly to SharePoint. These forms must be published to a network location and then uploaded to InfoPath Form Services.

To upload a form to InfoPath Form Services, follow these steps:

1. Launch Central Administration

2. Click General Application Settings.

3. Click the Upload Form Template link under the InfoPath Form Services section. The Upload Form Template page appears, as shown in Figure 19.7.

4. Click the Browse button to locate the form.

5. Optionally, click Verify to verify the form can be uploaded without any conflicts or errors.

6. Leave the Upgrade selection checked to upgrade any existing forms. If you uncheck this option, the new form will replace any existing form.

7. Leave the Allow Existing Sessions to Complete option selected so that users are not interrupted. Otherwise, select the Terminate option to essentially end all current user sessions.

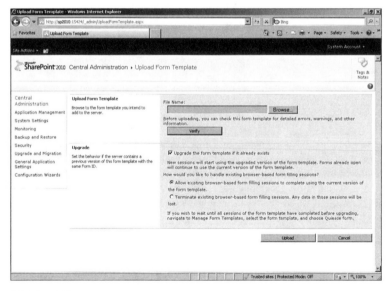

FIGURE 19.7
The Upload Form Template page allows you upload a form to InfoPath Form Services.

> **TIP** Terminating existing sessions is harsh in a production environment and might cause user frustration. It is always good practice to allow existing sessions to complete. An alternative option is to quiesce the form first, which allows all sessions to end but doesn't allow any new sessions to initiate.

What Happens When a Form Is Uploaded?

When a form is uploaded, it generates a feature for your SharePoint farm. The feature files are generated in the SharePoint 14 hive under TEMPLATESFEATURES, as shown in Figure 19.8. The feature folder is prefixed with FT for form-template.

FIGURE 19.8
Uploading a form generates a feature folder.

The feature is deployed globally to your site collections and can be activated just like any other feature. The form feature appears in the Site Collection Features list, as shown in Figure 19.9.

FIGURE 19.9
The form feature is available as a site collection feature.

Manage Form Templates

Scenario/Problem: You need to manage the form templates.

Solution: Click the Manage Form Templates link under the InfoPath Form Services section.

After forms are uploaded, they can be managed within the Manage Form Templates page. Selecting a form's drop-down menu shows the various actions available, as shown in Figure 19.10.

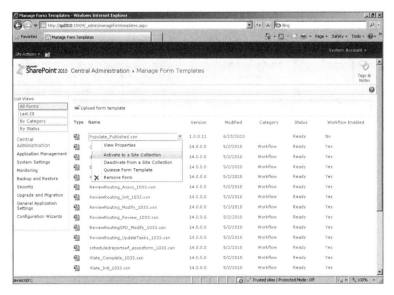

FIGURE 19.10
Each form can be managed by selecting the actions in its drop-down menu.

The actions available are as follows:

▷ **View Properties:** Displays all the information pertaining to the form.

▷ **Activate to a Site Collection:** When you upload a form, it generates and deploys a feature for your form to each site collection in your farm. This action activates that feature on the site collection you choose.

▷ **Deactivate from a Site Collection:** This action deactivates the form feature of the selected site collection.

▷ **Quiesce Form Template:** This action will halt the initiation of new form instances and allow existing user sessions to complete.

▷ **Remove Form:** This action deletes the form from InfoPath Forms Services.

TIP   Removing a form does not remove the content type it generates. Make sure the form is not being used anywhere in SharePoint. Otherwise, errors will occur when SharePoint tries to access the form template via the content type. (Hint: Remove the content type first, because SharePoint will notify if it is being used.)

What Happens When a Form Is Activated to a Site Collection?

When a form is activated to a site collection, the site collection feature for the form is activated, as shown in Figure 19.11. The form is now available as a content type in your form library, as shown in Figure 19.12.

See the "Use Multiple Forms in SharePoint Libraries" section in Chapter 8, "Submitting and Publishing in SharePoint," for more information about content types.

FIGURE 19.11
Activating a form activates the site collection feature.

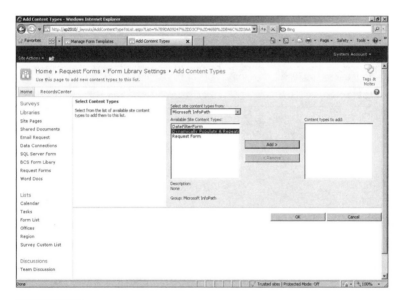

FIGURE 19.12
Activating the site collection features allows the form to be used as a content type.

Enable the Web Service Proxy

Scenario/Problem: You need to enable the use of the InfoPath Form Services Web Service Proxy.

Solution: Enable the proxy settings on the Configure InfoPath Form Services Web Service Proxy page.

The InfoPath Form Services web services proxy can be used to access web services without passing the credentials of the form user. A set of credentials for the web service need to be stored within SharePoint's Secure Store service (SSS), which is the replacement for Single Sign-On (SSO).

A data connection file that your InfoPath form is using as a web service connection simply needs to be modified by adding a UseFormsServiceProxy attribute with a setting of "true" along with an Authentication element that references the Secure Store application ID. If the UseFormsServiceProxy already exists, make sure the value is set to "true".

LISTING 19.1 **UseFormsServiceProxy Attribute**

```
<udc:ServiceUrl UseFormsServiceProxy="true"/>
```

LISTING 19.2 **Authentication Element**

```
<udc:Authentication>
    <udc:SSO AppId="<<AppID>>" CredentialType="<<credential type>>"/>
</udc:Authentication>
```

The possible credential types are as follows:

▶ Basic

▶ CD

▶ Digest

▶ Kerberos

▶ NTLM

▶ SQL

To enable the use of the web proxy, from Central Administration, General Application Settings, click the Configure InfoPath Form Services Web Service Proxy link under the InfoPath Form Services section. Enable the proxy settings, as shown in Figure 19.13.

> **NOTE** To use the SSS Service, InfoPath Forms Services needs to be configured to allow user form templates to use authentication information contained in data connection files.

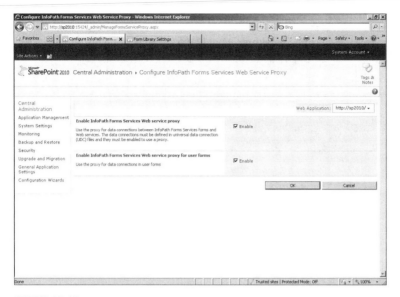

FIGURE 19.13
Checking the options enables InfoPath Form Services to use the web service proxy.

Manage Data Connections

Scenario/Problem: You need to manage data connections.

Solution: Click the Manage Data Connection Files link under the InfoPath Form Services section.

Central data connection files can be managed within the Manage Data Connections Files page. Selecting a file's drop-down menu shows the various actions available, as shown in Figure 19.14.

The actions available are as follows:

▶ **Edit Properties:** Displays the modifiable properties of the data connection files

▶ **Delete:** Removes the data connection file from the centrally managed data connections

TIP Common practice is to use data connection files within the specific site collection libraries (not using centrally managed data connections). However, common data connection files can be easily managed using the InfoPath Forms Services data connection repository.

FIGURE 19.14
Each data connection file can be managed by selecting the actions in its drop-down menu.

CHAPTER 20

PowerShell

This chapter discusses the administrative aspects of InfoPath Form Services through the use of PowerShell. PowerShell is the replacement for the previous STSADM console application. SharePoint 2010 provides a PowerShell Management Console that loads all the SharePoint-related functions into memory, thus providing an easy-to-use command-line interface.

Access SharePoint 2010 Management Shell

Scenario/Problem: You want to access the SharePoint 2010 Management Shell.

Solution: On any SharePoint server in your farm, select the SharePoint 2010 Management Shell program from the Start menu.

You can launch PowerShell and load the SharePoint module or just launch the SharePoint 2010 Management Shell. Launching the SharePoint 2010 Management Shell makes it easier to use PowerShell commands for SharePoint/InfoPath administration.

On any SharePoint server in your farm, select Start, All Programs, Microsoft Sharepoint 2010 Products, and then select the SharePoint 2010 Management Shell, as shown in Figure 20.1. The PowerShell command prompt window loads, as shown in Figure 20.2.

From here, you can enter any commands presented in this chapter to facilitate the configuration of InfoPath Form Services.

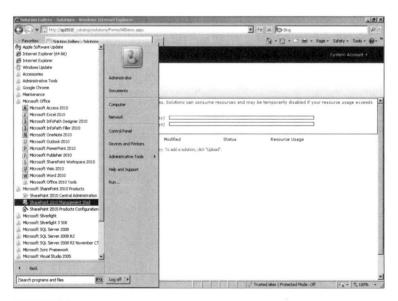

FIGURE 20.1
Selecting the SharePoint 2010 Management Shell loads PowerShell with the SharePoint module.

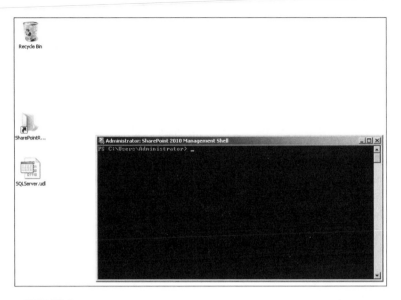

FIGURE 20.2
Launching the SharePoint 2010 Management Shell loads the PowerShell command prompt window.

Browser-Enable Form Templates

Scenario/Problem: You need to allow custom SharePoint forms to be rendered within SharePoint.

Solution: Use the Set-SPInfoPathFormsService command.

From the PowerShell command prompt, enter the following:

```
Set-SPInfoPathFormsService -AllowUserFormBrowserEnabling $true
-AllowUserFormBrowserRendering $true
```

TIP To disable the browser-enabled form templates, replace $true with $false.

Throttle Data Connection Timeouts

Scenario/Problem: You need to increase or decrease the data connection timeout limit.

Solution: Use the Set-SPInfoPathFormsService command with the data connection timeout parameters.

Your form will attempt to connect and access data sources based on your configured data connections. If the data source is not accessible, busy, or down, InfoPath Forms Services needs a way to time out the connection such that the form or the browser doesn't stop responding.

Use the -DefaultDataConnectionTimeout and -MaxDataConnectionTimeout parameters with the Set-SPInfoPathFormsService command to set the timeout values, as shown in Listing 20.1.

LISTING 20.1 **Data Connection Timeout Command Line**

```
Set-SPInfoPathFormsService -DefaultDataConnectionTimeout 15000 -
MaxDataConnectionTimeout 25000
```

TIP The default values are usually acceptable entries and do not need to modified. However, if you have some long-running data processes or connectivity issues, you may want to increase these numbers slightly.

Throttle the Data Connection Response Size

Scenario/Problem: You need to increase or decrease the data connection response size.

Solution: Use the MaxDataConnectionResponseSize parameter with the Set-SPInfoPathFormsService command.

When connecting to data sources, you do not want to overload other systems. Limiting the response size determines how many kilobytes the data connection can process. You can modify the setting by using the MaxDataConnectionReponseSize parameter with the number of kilobytes, as shown in Listing 20.2.

LISTING 20.1 **Data Connection Timeout Command Line**

```
Set-SPInfoPathFormsService -MaxDataConnectionResponseSize 3000
```

> **TIP** The default value of 1500KB is usually a good setting. You do not want to strain other systems or databases. This also helps limit traffic on the network. Only increase this value if you have a large form that submits a great deal of data.

Modify Authentication Settings

Scenario/Problem: You need to modify authentication settings.

Solution: Use the Set-SPInfoPathFormsService command with the appropriate parameters.

Several data authentication options are available that either allow or prohibit certain types of data connectivity, as follows:

> ▶ **RequireSslForDataConnections:** Set this option to true to require SSL encryption when your form uses HTTP authentication (such as when accessing a web service).

> ▶ **AllowEmbeddedSqlForDataConnection:** Set this option to true if you have data connection files which contain SQL database connection information including the username and password.

> ▶ **AllowUdcAuthenticationForDataConnections:** Set this option to true to allow custom forms to access data sources through data connection files.

> ▶ **AllowUserFormCrossDomainDataConnections:** Select this option if your form needs to access data sources on a different domain than SharePoint.

To configure these settings, use the Set-SPInfoPathFormsService command with the desired parameters and settings, as shown in Listing 20.3.

LISTING 20.3 **Authentication Settings Command Line**

```
Set-SPInfoPathFormsService -RequireSslForDataConnections $true -
AllowEmbeddedSqlForDataConnection $true -
AllowUdcAuthenticationForDataConnections $true -
AllowUserFormCrossDomainDataConnections $true
```

Configure Session State

Scenario/Problem: You want to configure session state settings.

Solution: Use the Set-SPInfoPathFormsService command with the appropriate parameters.

When a user is filling out a SharePoint form, InfoPath Form Services uses the SharePoint Server State service to manage user sessions. (You can switch this to View State using PowerShell; see the next section.) Transient data is stored within the session state.

There are several settings involved in the session state configuration:

- ▶ **MaxPostbacksPerSession:** Typically, there shouldn't be too much chatter between the form and Forms Services. This setting prevents unintended postbacks or "out-of-control" communications.

- ▶ **MaxUserActionsPerPostback:** There should be only a handful of actions per postback. Once again, this is prevent a form process from pegging server resources.

- ▶ **ActiveSessionTimeout:** By default, active sessions are terminated after 1,440 minutes, which essentially is 24 hours. This is more of a cleanup process than anything. Some forms may take a long time to fill out depending on the information required, but one day should be plenty of time.

- ▶ **MaxSizeOfFormSessionState:** This determines how much data can be stored for the active user session. The default is 4096KB, which equates to 4MB. This provides plenty of room to store user session data. Typical forms and user information should only take up several kilobytes if not bytes.

If the user session lasts too long or there too many postbacks to the server, the session is ended based on the configured settings. All form data will be lost, and the user will need to start over. This is done to prevent unintended communication, limit network traffic, and limit system resource utilization.

To configure these settings, use the Set-SPInfoPathFormsService command with the desired parameters and settings, as shown in Listing 20.4.

LISTING 20.4 **Session State Settings Command Line**

```
Set-SPInfoPathFormsService -MaxPostbacksPerSession 100 -
ActiveSessionTimeout 720
```

TIP If forms are constantly being filled out within your organization and are fairly lightweight, you might actually want to reduce some of these values to keep recycling the session state as well as system resources. Another option is to use View State instead, as described in the next section.

Enable View State

Scenario/Problem: Instead of using Session State, you would like to use View State.

Solution: Use the AllowViewState parameter with the Set-SPInfoPathFormsService command.

View State sessions (or Form View) store session data within the client browser, thus reducing load on the database server. Although this assists in maximizing database performance, there is more bandwidth used in View State than in Session State. The maximum session size allowed in the View State is 40KB. If there is an instance where this limit is passed, the session automatically switches back to Session State.

To configure these settings, use the Set-SPInfoPathFormsService command with the -AllowViewState and -ViewStateThreshold parameters, as shown in Listing 20.5.

LISTING 20.5 **ViewState State Settings Command Line**

```
Set-SPInfoPathFormsService -AllowViewState $true -ViewStateThreshold
40961
```

TIP You can only modify this setting using the PowerShell command line. There are no equivalent options in Central Administration.

Verify and Upload a Form Template

Scenario/Problem: You need to verify and upload a form template to InfoPath Form Services.

Solution: Use the Test-SPInfoPathFormTemplate and Install-SPInfoPathFormTemplate PowerShell commands to verify and upload the form template.

Forms that have code-behind or that require Full Trust permissions cannot be published directly to SharePoint. These forms must be published to a network location and then uploaded to Form Services. Before uploading, you should verify that the form is correct and can be installed.

To verify a form template, use the following command:

```
Test-SPInfoPathFormTemplate -Path "<<full path to InfoPath form
template>>"
```

To upload a form to InfoPath Form Services, use the following command:

```
Install-SPInfoPathFormTemplate -Path "<<full path to InfoPath form
template>>"
```

> **TIP** Use the switch parameter -EnableGradualUpgrade with the Install-SPInfoPathFormTemplate to ensure that existing forms are upgraded.

Upload Multiple Form Templates at Once

> **Scenario/Problem:** You have many form templates to upload to InfoPath Form Services but find it difficult performing the same process for each one individually.

Solution: Pipe the paths of all form templates you want to upload to the Install-SPInfoPathFormTemplate command.

You may upload multiple form templates by listing out each path separated by a comma and then using the pipe (|) to pass that list into the Install-SPInfoPathFormTemplate command, as shown in Listing 20.6

LISTING 20.6 **Multiple-Form Upload Command Line**

```
"<<path of form 1>>" , "<<path of form 2>>" , "<<path of form 3>>" |
Install-SPInfoPathFormTemplate
```

Activate or Deactivate a Form to a Site Collection

> **Scenario/Problem:** You need to activate or deactivate a form to a site collection.

Solution: Use the Enable-SPInfoPathFormTemplate or Disable-SPInfoPathFormTemplate commands.

When you upload a form, it generates and deploys a feature for your form to each site collection in your farm. Using the Enable-SPInfoPathFormTemplate command activates that feature on the site collection you choose. Conversely, using the Disable-SPInfoPathFormTemplate command deactivates the form feature of the selected site collection.

To activate a form to a site collection, use the following command:

```
Enable-SPInfoPathFormTemplate -Identity "<<name of form template>>" -Site
"<<URL of Site Collection>>"
```

To deactivate a form from a site collection, use the following command:

```
Disable-SPInfoPathFormTemplate -Identity "<<name of form template>>"
-Site "<<URL of Site Collection>>"
```

Remove a Form from InfoPath Form Services

Scenario/Problem: You need to remove a form from InfoPath Form Services.

Solution: Use the Uninstall-SPInfoPathFormTemplate PowerShell command.

Removing a form deletes the form from InfoPath Forms Services. It is no longer available on any site collection. To remove a form from InfoPath Form Services, use the following command:

```
Uninstall-SPInfoPathFormTemplate -Identity "<<name of form template>>"
```

TIP Removing a form does not always remove the content type it generates. Make sure the form is not being used anywhere in SharePoint. Otherwise, errors will occur when SharePoint tries to access the form template via the content type. (Hint: Remove the content type first as SharePoint will notify if it is being used.)

Quiesce a Form from InfoPath Form Services

Scenario/Problem: You need to quiesce a form from InfoPath Form Services.

Solution: Use the Stop-SPInfoPathFormTemplate PowerShell command.

Quiescing a form will halt the initiation of new form instances and allow existing user sessions to complete. To quiesce a form from InfoPath Form Services, use the following command:

```
Stop-SPInfoPathFormTemplate -Identity "<<name of form template>>"
```

Enable the Web Service Proxy

Scenario/Problem: You need to enable the use of the InfoPath Form Services web service proxy.

Solution: Use the Set-SPInfoPathWebServiceProxy command.

The InfoPath Form Services web services proxy can be used to access web services without passing the credentials of the form user. A set of credentials for the web service need to be stored within SharePoint's Secure Store service (SSS), which is the replacement for Single Sign-On (SSO).

A data connection file that your InfoPath form is using as a web service connection simply needs to be modified by adding a UseFormsServiceProxy attribute with a setting of "true" along with an Authentication element that references the Secure Store application ID.

LISTING 20.7 **UseFormsServiceProxy Attribute**

```
<udc:ServiceUrl UseFormsServiceProxy="true"/>
```

LISTING 20.8 **Authentication Element**

```
<udc:Authentication>
    <udc:SSO AppId="<<AppID>>" CredentialType="<<credential type>>"/>
</udc:Authentication>
```

The possible credential types are as follows:

- Basic
- CD
- Digest
- Kerberos
- NTLM
- SQL

To enable the use of the web proxy, use the following command:

```
Set-SPInfoPathWebServiceProxy -Identity "<<URL of web application>>"
-AllowWebServiceProxy $true
```

To enable SharePoint forms to use the web proxy, use the following command:

```
Set-SPInfoPathWebServiceProxy -Identity "<<URL of web application>>"
-AllowForUserForms $true
```

TIP The AllowWebServiceProxy setting needs to be set to true first before AllowForUserForms can be set to true. This is why the commands need to be separated.

CHAPTER 21

Managing Form Permissions

IN THIS CHAPTER

- ▶ Create Unique Permissions on a Form Library
- ▶ Grant Users Permissions
- ▶ Create a Permission Level for Your Form Library
- ▶ Edit a Group's Permission Level
- ▶ Create a Submit-Only Permission Level

This chapter explores the administrative aspects of managing form permissions within SharePoint. The proper permissions determine who can access the forms and what kind of rights they have.

Users/groups need a permission level that contains the Add Items permission such that they may submit a form or save a list item. The Edit Items permission is required if you need to allow users/groups to edit existing items in the library or list. For general viewing of your forms or list items, the View Items permission is needed.

Create Unique Permissions on a Form Library

Scenario/Problem: You have a form library that needs unique permissions.

Solution: Break inheritance from the parent site.

The first level of permissions for your forms starts at the site level. When you create a new form library, the library inherits the permissions of the site in which it was created. Therefore, to begin managing permissions of your forms, you first need to break inheritance from the site. To do this, follow these steps:

1. Navigate to your form library in SharePoint.

2. From the Library ribbon, click the Library Permissions button, as shown in Figure 21.1, to manage the form library's permissions.

3. On the Permissions screen, click Stop Inheriting Permissions from the Edit ribbon to break inheritance from the parent site, as shown in Figure 21.2.

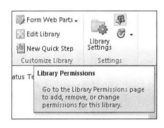

FIGURE 21.1
Clicking the Library Permissions button allows you to manage the form library's permissions.

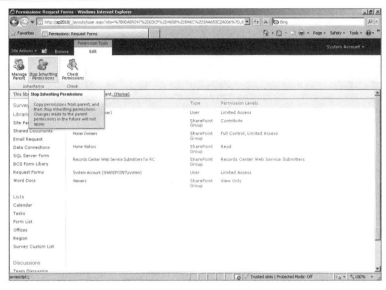

FIGURE 21.2
Clicking Stop Inheriting Permissions breaks inheritance from the parent site.

Grant Users Permissions

Scenario/Problem: You need to allow users to access your forms.

Solution: Add users to a group that has access to the form library.

The best practice for managing permissions is to grant the permissions to groups and then add the appropriate users to those groups. This allows you to easily manage who has access to your form library, because you need to worry only about the group access and not each individual user; if the users are in the group, they have that group's access level.

To grant permissions on your form library after you have broken inheritance, click the Grant Permissions button on the Permission page, as shown in Figure 21.3.

Select the users within the Users/Groups box, and then select the group they should be added as shown in Figure 21.4. You may also grant the users permissions directly by selecting the Grant Users Permission Directly option.

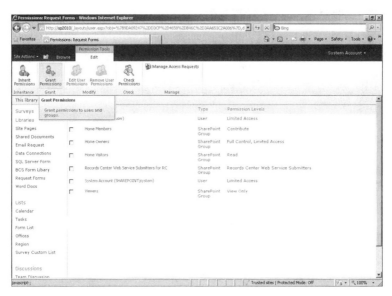

FIGURE 21.3

Clicking Grant Permissions allows you to add users or groups to your form library.

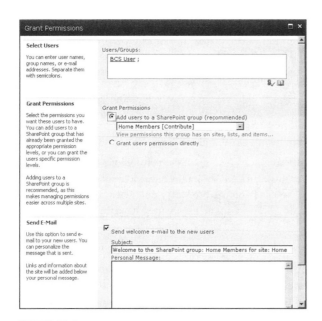

FIGURE 21.4

Adding a user to the group grants them the group's permission.

TIP   Create a new site-level group specifically for your forms library so that you do not need to give users permissions through the main site groups.

Create a Permission Level for Your Form Library

Scenario/Problem: You only want to provide the permissions necessary for your form library.

Solution: Create a custom permission level in the site and use that to grant users/ groups permissions in your form library.

Granting users/groups Contribute rights to your form library is a surefire way to allow them to read, add, and edit items. However, this permission level also allows the users to delete the items which may not be desired. Therefore, I recommend creating a custom permission level that contains only the permissions needed on the form library. The permission level is created in the site but may be applied within your form library permissions.

To create a custom permission level, follow these steps:

1. Navigate to your root SharePoint site.

2. From the Site Actions menu, select Site Permissions to access the Permissions page of the site, as shown in Figure 21.5.

3. On the Permissions page, click Permission Levels from the Edit ribbon, as shown in Figure 21.6, to manage the site's permission levels.

FIGURE 21.5
Selecting Site Permissions accesses the Permissions page of the site.

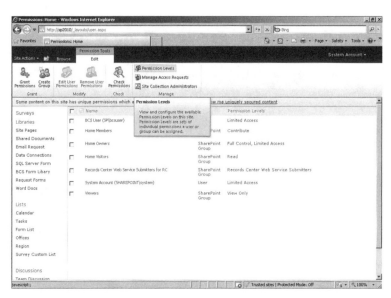

FIGURE 21.6
Clicking Permission Levels allows you to manage the site's permission levels.

4. Click the Add a Permission Level link at the top of the page. The Add a Permission Level page appears.

5. Enter a name for the permission level and select the appropriate permissions, as shown in Figure 21.7.

6. Click Create.

The permission level is created, and now you may use that to grant users/groups custom permissions without using the system-based permission levels such as Contribute. See the next section for steps on applying this level to your groups.

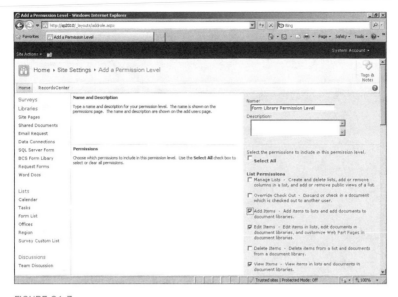

FIGURE 21.7
Selecting the permissions configures the custom permission level.

Edit a Group's Permission Level

Scenario/Problem: You need to edit an existing group's permission level within your form library.

Solution: Edit the group's permissions from the library's permissions page.

Whether you created a custom permission level from the previous section or need to modify a group's permissions, you can easily edit the assigned permission levels by following these steps:

1. Navigate to your form library.

2. Click Library Permissions from the Library ribbon.

3. Select a user or group and click the Edit User Permissions button, as shown in Figure 21.8, to configure the assigned permission levels. The Edit Permissions dialog appears.

4. Select the desired permissions in the Choose Permissions section of the Edit Permissions dialog, as shown in Figure 21.9, to configure the permission levels applied to the selected user/group.

FIGURE 21.8
Clicking the Edit User Permissions button allows you to configure the assigned permission levels.

> **NOTE** In addition to the normal Add Items, Edit Items, and other permissions, the View Application Pages and Use Client Integration Features permissions are required for users to interact and use InfoPath forms within SharePoint 2010.

5. Click OK.

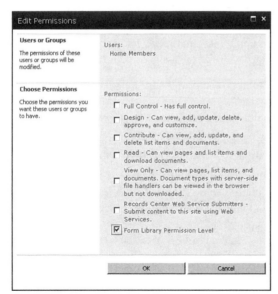

FIGURE 21.9
Choosing the permissions configures the levels applied to the selected user or group.

Create a Submit-Only Permission Level

Scenario/Problem: You want to create a submit-only permission level.

Solution: Add a permission level using a custom console application that provides only the Add Items permission.

There may be certain cases where you want a user to submit a form but not see any contents of the form library (not even their own submission). Several business scenarios may require this (for example, a suggestion form).

When creating a custom permission level from within SharePoint, selecting Add Items automatically selects View Items. Unchecking View Items unchecks the Add Items. So there seems to be no way to have only the Add Items permission without the View Items permission.

You can, however, achieve this by using code within a console application. The console application should take three arguments: the site collection URL, the name of the permission, and a description. These are the required variables for the permission code as shown in Listing 21.1. The code to perform the creation of the permission is shown in Listing 21.2.

LISTING 21.1 **Permission Variables**

```
string siteCollectionURL = args[0];
string nameOfPermissionLevel = args[1];
string description = args[2];
```

LISTING 21.2 **Creating the Permission**

```
using (SPSite oSiteCollection = new SPSite(siteCollectionURL))
{
  using (SPWeb oWebsite = oSiteCollection.OpenWeb())
  {
    if (!oWebsite.HasUniqueRoleDefinitions)
    {
      oWebsite.RoleDefinitions.BreakInheritance(true, true);
    }

    SPRoleDefinition oRoleDefinition = new SPRoleDefinition();
    oRoleDefinition.Name = nameOfPermissionLevel;
    oRoleDefinition.Description = description;
    oRoleDefinition.BasePermissions = SPBasePermissions.AddListItems &
SPBasePermissions.ViewFormPages & SPBasePermissions.UseClientIntegration;
    oWebsite.RoleDefinitions.Add(oRoleDefinition);
  }
}
```

Package the required code into a console application and compile the executable. Run the executable on one of your servers in the SharePoint farm. An example command line execution is as follows:

```
createpermissionlevel.exe "http://sp2010 " "Submit Only" "Allow users to
only submit"
```

The new permission level is created, and you may now use that to create a Submit-Only permission level. You may also perform the same operation using PowerShell as shown in Listing 22.3.

LISTING 21.3 PowerShell Commands for Submit Only Permission Level

```
$web = get-spweb "http://sp2010"
$newroledef = New-Object "Microsoft.SharePoint.SPRoleDefinition"
$newroledef.Name = "Submit Only"
$newroledef.Description = "Allow users to only submit a form but not view
or edit"
$newroledef.BasePermissions = "AddListItems,ViewFormPages,UseClientInteg
ration"
$web.RoleDefinitions.Add($newroledef)
$web.Update()
```

> **NOTE** Because the View Items permission is not assigned, you will need to control the launching and closing of the form such that SharePoint does not return to the form library where the form is submitted. You might experience errors otherwise.

CHAPTER 22

General Form Issues

This chapter explores various form issues that may arise during your SharePoint form development and suggests possible resolutions. It is suggested to browse through all the troubleshooting chapters to become aware of potential pitfalls.

Resolve: Issue Accessing Data Source

Scenario/Problem: An error occurred when querying a data source.

Solution: Follow troubleshooting steps.

This is one of the most common errors messages to receive, as shown in Figure 22.1, and means a problem exists with the data connection or data source itself.

You can take several troubleshooting steps, as follows:

1. Ensure that the data source is available and reachable.

2. Make sure the data connection file exists in the data connection library.

3. Make sure the data connection file has been approved in the data connection library. If the status is pending, that could be the issue.

4. Make sure the permissions on the data sources, lists, libraries, and data connection files are correct.

5. Review the contents of the data connection file to insure the configuration is correct including any credentials.

6. Always click Show Details (if presented) to glean more informative debugging ammunition.

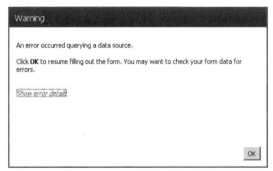

FIGURE 22.1
Any issue with a data connection produces this error.

7. Investigate the event log on the server to uncover any other issues.

Resolve: SQL Credential Issue

Scenario/Problem: The event log has an exception stating "Current configuration settings prohibit embedding username and password in the database connection string" as shown in Figure 22.2.

Solution: Within the InfoPath Form Services settings, check the Allow Embedded SQL Authentication option.

From Central Administration, follow these steps:

1. Click the General Application Settings link on the left-side navigation.

2. Under InfoPath Form Services, click the Configure InfoPath Form Services link.

3. On the Configure InfoPath Form Service page, check the Allow Embedded SQL Authentication option, as shown in Figure 22.3.

4. Click OK.

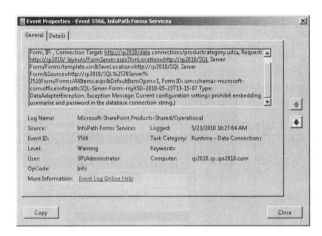

FIGURE 22.2
Not allowing embedded credentials produces this event log entry.

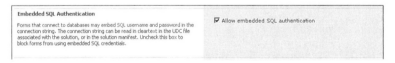

FIGURE 22.3
Checking the Allow Embedded SQL Authentication option resolves the exception error.

Resolve: Business Data Connectivity Metadata Store Is Currently Unavailable

Scenario/Problem: You are in SharePoint Designer and you attempt to review the external content types to obtain connection information, but you receive a message stating that the Business Data Connectivity Metadata Store is currently unavailable.

Solution: Start the Business Data Connectivity Service on the server using Central Administration.

FIGURE 22.4
When the Business Data Connectivity Service is not started, you will receive this message in SharePoint Designer.

The Business Data Connectivity Service is probably not started on the server and therefore needs to be started. To do this, follow these steps:

1. Open SharePoint 2010 Central Administration.

2. Under System Settings, click the Manage services on server link.

3. Find the Business Data Connectivity Service line and click the Start link, as shown in Figure 22.5.

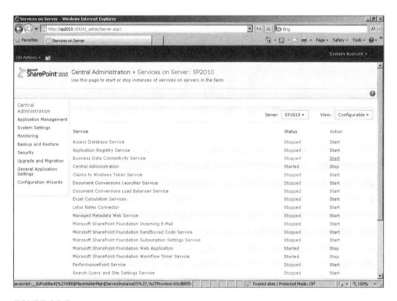

FIGURE 22.5
Clicking the Start link starts the Business Data Connectivity Service.

Resolve: Picker Issue Obtaining Business Data

Scenario/Problem: You are previewing a form that contains an external content picker control. When you attempt to select an external item, an error message appears in the dialog stating that an error occurred obtaining business data using the picker web service.

Solution: Publish your form to SharePoint and test the form within the browser.

When you use an external item picker on a SharePoint form, the control is configured to connect to the data source through SharePoint. Therefore, when attempting to preview the form, you receive a message in the picker dialog, as shown in Figure 22.6.

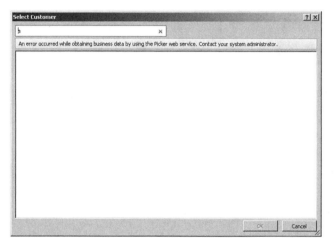

FIGURE 22.6
Previewing an external item picker produces this error when configured to connect through SharePoint.

You need to publish the form to SharePoint and test the connection there because the control is configured to connect through SharePoint itself.

Resolve: Modifying a List/Library Page Makes the Ribbon Disappear

Scenario/Problem: After you modify a list page by adding additional web parts, the List or Library ribbon is no longer presented.

Solution: Select the List or Library web part on the page, and the ribbon will be presented.

The List/Library ribbon is contextual based on the current objects on the page. By default, only the List or Library web part exists and therefore the ribbon appears. When you modify a list or library page, the context is changed, as shown in Figure 22.7.

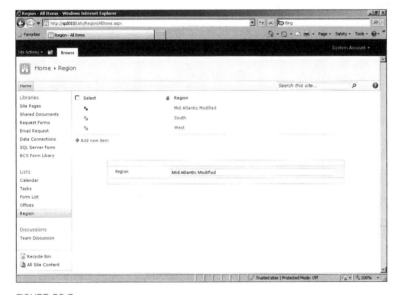

FIGURE 22.7
Modifying the page causes the ribbon to disappear.

Once the List or Library web part on the page is selected, the ribbon is displayed accordingly, as shown in Figure 22.8.

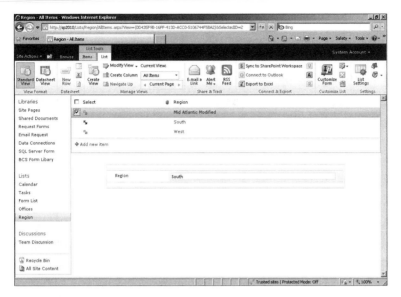

FIGURE 22.8
Selecting the List web part on the page produces the List ribbon.

Resolve: SharePoint Designer Task List Creation Error

Scenario/Problem: You are creating a workflow in SharePoint Designer for your SharePoint form. While creating a new task, you receive a message that the task list already exists.

Solution: Either you need to remove the existing task list or use a different name.

When you are creating a new task, such as a to-do item, SharePoint Designer generates a content type with the name you enter. Therefore, if you attempt to use the same name, a message appears as shown in Figure 22.9.

FIGURE 22.9
Entering a task name that was already used produces this message.

If the original content type is not being used by another workflow or process, remove the content type from your site and attempt to create the task item again. Otherwise, provide a different name for the task.

Resolve: VSTA Required Issue

Scenario/Problem: You attempt to use the Code Editor or create an event for your form, and you receive a message that states that Microsoft Visual Studio Tools for Applications (VSTA) is required.

Solution: Install VSTA from the Office 2010 installation.

To produce code within your form, you need to have VSTA installed on your machine. This is not installed automatically during the Office 2010 installation (or InfoPath 2010 installation). You will receive the error shown in Figure 22.10 if you do not have VSTA.

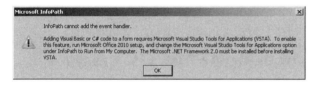

FIGURE 22.10
Not having VSTA installed produces this message when attempting to create code in your form.

To resolve this issue, follow these steps:

1. Close InfoPath Designer 2010.

2. Open the Control Panel.

3. Click Programs and Features.

4. Select the Microsoft Office 2010 entry and click Change.

5. Keep Add or Remove Features selected and click Continue.

6. On the Installation Options dialog, expand Microsoft InfoPath.

7. Expand .NET Programmability Support under Microsoft InfoPath.

8. Click the drop-down item menu on the Visual Studio for Applications entry and select Run from My Computer, as shown in Figure 22.11.

9. Click Continue. The VSTA is installed.

10. Open InfoPath Designer 2010 and click Code Editor on the Developer ribbon to ensure that you are able to produce code and event handlers.

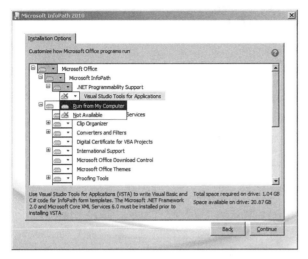

FIGURE 22.11
Changing the Visual Studio Tools for Applications to Run from My Computer installs the necessary files.

TIP   Sometimes just installing VSTA does not resolve the issue, especially on a virtual machine running a Windows Server product. A surefire way to allow VSTA to run is to select the Microsoft Office drop-down menu and select Run All from My Computer.

Resolve: Error Loading the Form

Scenario/Problem: In SharePoint, while you are attempting to create a new form, an error loading the form message appears. The form previously rendered and was working fine.

Solution: Remove the content type from SharePoint, redeploy the form, or activate it to the site collection.

When a form is deployed as a content type either directly or through InfoPath Forms Services but then the form is removed or deactivated from the site collection, the content type still exists.

Because the content type still exists, when you attempt to create a new document using the form content type, SharePoint cannot find the form template. The error shown in Figure 22.12 is produced.

If the form should no longer be used, make sure you remove the content type from SharePoint so that there is no reference to the deleted form. If the form is still being used, redeploy the form or make sure the form is activated on the site collection.

FIGURE 22.12
Removing a form template from InfoPath Forms Services produces this error when attempting to create a new instance.

Resolve: Security Exception Using Code-Behind

Scenario/Problem: When previewing or rendering a form that contains code-behind, you receive a security exception.

Solution: Change the form's security setting to Full Trust.

When your form needs to execute code and the security setting is not configured, you receive an error message similar to Figure 22.13.

To resolve this issue, follow these steps:

1. Click File, Info.

2. Click the Form Options button. The Form Options dialog appears.

3. Select the Security and Trust category from the list on the left.

4. Uncheck the Automatically Determine Security Level check box. The security-level options are enabled.

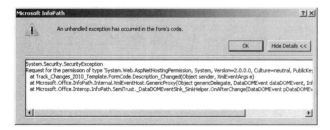

FIGURE 22.13
Not setting a form's security to Full Trust produces this security exception.

5. Select the Full Trust option.

6. Click OK.

CHAPTER 23

Deployment and Publishing Issues

This chapter explores various issues that may arise during the deployment and publishing of a SharePoint form and suggests possible resolutions. It is suggested to browse through all the troubleshooting chapters to become aware of potential pitfalls.

Resolve: No File with URL in This Web

Scenario/Problem: You attempt to publish your form to a SharePoint location but receive an error that states no file with URL in this web.

Solution: Correct the URL location and republish.

When the path you enter does not exist within your SharePoint site, you receive a message similar to Figure 23.1.

To resolve this issue, follow these steps:

1. Click OK on the error message.

2. Verify the URL entered.

3. Go back through the Publishing Wizard to correct the form location.

4. Continue with normal publishing procedures.

FIGURE 23.1
Entering an invalid URL produces this error when publishing.

TIP Open your SharePoint site to verify the proper locations. Review the URL in the browser. In the example, FormTemplates was used. But when you navigate to the Form Templates library on the site, the URL location is named FormServerTemplates.

Resolve: Form Cannot Be Browser-Enabled on Selected Site

Scenario/Problem: You attempt to publish your form to SharePoint. The Publishing Wizard displays a message informing you that the form cannot be browser-enabled on the selected site.

Solution: Configure InfoPath Forms Services to allow browser-enabled forms.

When browser-enabled forms are not enabled within InfoPath Form Services, the Publishing Wizard displays a message, as shown in Figure 23.2.

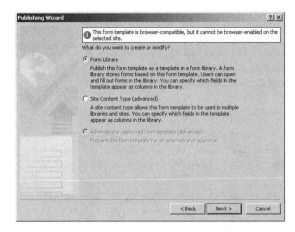

FIGURE 23.2
The Publishing Wizard displays this message when browser forms are not enabled.

To resolve this issue, follow these steps:

1. Launch SharePoint 2010 Central Administration.

2. Click the General Application Settings link on the left-side navigation.

3. Under InfoPath Form Services, click the Configure InfoPath Form Services link.

4. On the Configure InfoPath Form Service page, check the User Browser-Enabled Form Templates check boxes, as shown in Figure 22.3.

5. Click OK.

FIGURE 23.3
Checking the browser-enabled check boxes allows the form to be published and rendered as a SharePoint form.

Resolve: Form Template Has Not Been Published

Scenario/Problem: You attempt to upload your form template into InfoPath Forms Services but receive an error stating that the form has not been published.

Solution: Publish the form as an administrator-approved form and upload the published version.

When developing a form that will be uploaded into InfoPath Forms Services at the farm level, the form needs to be published as an administrator-approved form. If you attempt to upload the form template, you will receive the error shown in Figure 23.4.

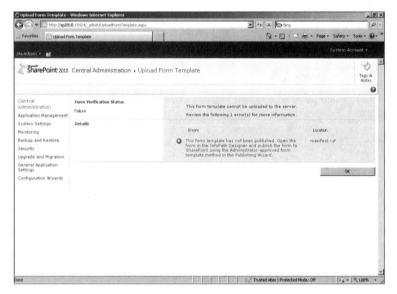

FIGURE 23.4
Checking the browser-enabled check boxes allows the form to be published and rendered as a SharePoint form.

You need to publish the form as an administrator-approved form using a network location or a different local location. Use the published version of the form to upload into InfoPath Forms Services.

Resolve: Sandboxed Solutions Not Enabled

Scenario/Problem: You attempt to publish your form containing code-behind directly to a form library on your SharePoint site and receive an error message stating that sandboxed solutions are not enabled.

Solution: Publish the form as an administrator-approved form and upload the published version.

Any form with code-behind needs to be published as an administrator-approved form and then uploaded to InfoPath Forms Services. If you attempt to publish directly to the SharePoint site, you receive an error, as shown in Figure 23.5.

FIGURE 23.5
Attempting to directly publish a form containing code to a form library produces this error.

Regardless of sandboxed solutions being enabled, because the form is not packaged as a solution (.wsp file), it cannot be deployed directly to SharePoint. The upload process of an administrator-approved form produces the appropriate feature solution when uploaded to InfoPath Form Services.

CHAPTER 24

Form Submission Issues

This chapter explores various issues that may arise during the submission of a SharePoint form and suggests possible resolutions. It is suggested to browse through all the troubleshooting chapters to become aware of potential pitfalls.

Troubleshoot General Submission Issues

Scenario/Problem: An error occurs when submitting a form.

Solution: Follow troubleshooting steps.

There are many reasons why a form cannot be submitted. Several detailed errors are explained in the following sections. However, there are several general troubleshooting steps to take, as follows:

1. Ensure that the data source used for submission is available and reachable.

2. Make sure the data connection file exists in the data connection library.

3. Make sure the data connection file has been approved in the data connection library. If the status is pending, that could be the issue.

4. Make sure the permissions on libraries, lists, and data connection files are correct.

5. Review the contents of the data connection file to ensure the configuration is correct, including any credentials.

6. Always click Show Details (if presented in the error message box) to glean more informative debugging ammunition.

7. Investigate the event log on the server to uncover any other issues.

Resolve: SharePoint Location Is Read-Only

Scenario/Problem: Upon submission of a form to SharePoint, an error occurs explaining the form cannot be submitted because the SharePoint location is read-only or you do not have permissions.

Solution: Verify that the user has permissions on the form library where the form is configured to be submitted.

To successfully submit a form to a form library, the user must have Contribute permissions. Otherwise, the user receives a message similar to Figure 24.1.

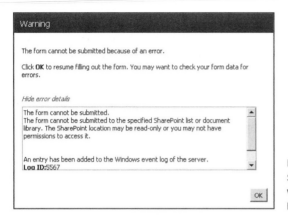

FIGURE 24.1
Submitting to a form library without proper permissions produces this error.

Resolve: Document Library Already Contains a File with the Same Name

Scenario/Problem: Upon submission of a form to SharePoint, an error occurs explaining the document library already contains a file with the same name.

Solution: Ensure that the submission data connection in your form is producing a unique form name or that the submission allows overwriting existing forms.

If the form does not use a unique name and the submission does not allow overwriting files, you will receive an error similar to Figure 24.2 when attempting to submit a form twice.

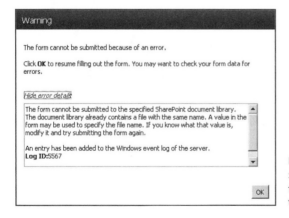

FIGURE 24.2
Submitting to a form library with a form of the same name produces this error.

During the configuration of the submit data connection, ensure that the filename being produced is unique to avoid any conflicts. See Chapter 2, "Creating a SharePoint Form with InfoPath Designer," for a discussion about using a filename formula.

Also, if your process allows the resubmission of the same form, ensure that you check the Allow Overwrite if File Exists check box, as shown in Figure 24.3.

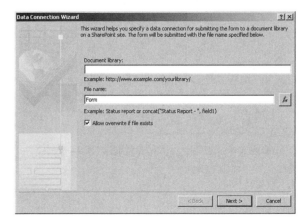

FIGURE 24.3
Check the Allow Overwrite if File Exists check box to allow a form to be resubmitted.

Resolve: Errors Submitting to a Web Service

Scenario/Problem: Upon submission of a form to a web service, you receive a SOAP error.

Solution: Follow the troubleshooting steps.

Submitting data to a web service requires that all expected values be provided and in the correct format. Otherwise, SOAP errors occur. as shown in Figure 24.4.

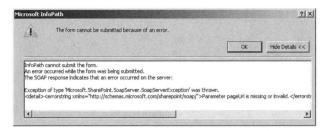

FIGURE 24.4
Submitting invalid data to a web service produces a SOAP error.

To investigate and resolve SOAP errors, follow these steps:

1. Ensure the web service is running. Open a web browser and attempt to reach the web service.

2. Ensure that all the expected parameters are being submitted with data from your form.

3. Ensure that the data types expected match with the data types from your form.

4. Some data elements may need to be submitted as a string. Check the Submit Data as a String check box, as shown in Figure 24.5.

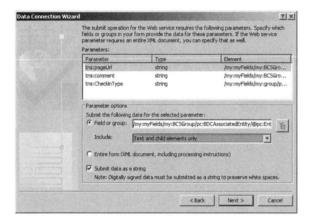

FIGURE 24.5
Some form data elements may need to be submitted as a string.

Index

A

The **How-To series** publishes titles with informative "how-to" information for each of its respective topic areas. The titles focus on detailing each step necessary to accomplish a goal for a given scenario.

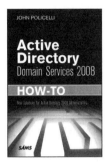

Active Directory Domain Services 2008 How-To
ISBN-13: 9780672330452

C# 4.0 How-To
ISBN-13: 9780672330636

Exchange Server 2007 How-To
ISBN-13: 9780672330483

Silverlight 4 How-To
ISBN-13: 9780672330629

SharePoint 2010 How-To
ISBN-13: 9780672333354

Windows Server 2008 How-To
ISBN-13: 9780672330759

How-To series books are available at most retail and online bookstores. For more information or to order direct, visit our online bookstore at **informit.com/store**

Online editions of all How-To series titles are available by subscription from Safari Books Online at **safari.informit.com**

FREE Online Edition

Your purchase of **InfoPath with SharePoint 2010 How-To** includes access to a free online edition for 45 days through the Safari Books Online subscription service. Nearly every Sams book is available online through Safari Books Online, along with more than 5,000 other technical books and videos from publishers such as Addison-Wesley Professional, Cisco Press, Exam Cram, IBM Press, O'Reilly, Prentice Hall, and Que.

SAFARI BOOKS ONLINE allows you to search for a specific answer, cut and paste code, download chapters, and stay current with emerging technologies.

Activate your FREE Online Edition at
www.informit.com/safarifree

> **STEP 1:** Enter the coupon code: EDLTREH.

> **STEP 2:** New Safari users, complete the brief registration form. Safari subscribers, just log in.

If you have difficulty registering on Safari or accessing the online edition, please e-mail customer-service@safaribooksonline.com